THIS BOOK BELONGS TO:

GO GIRL

A STORYBOOK OF EPIC NZ WOMEN

by Barbara Else

PUFFIN

Contents

Every girl can write her own story. Reach high and go, girl!

AHUMAI TE PAERATA • BEATRICE FAUMUINA
BEATRICE TINSLEY • ELIZABETH McCOMBS
CATHERINE TIZARD • FARAH PALMER
ELLA WILLIAMS • FRANCES HODGKINS
GEORGINA BEYER • FRAN HAYLEY WESTENRA
HELEN CLARK • HŪRIA MĀTENGA • INGRID VISSER
KATE SHEPPERD • JANE CAMPION
KATHERINE MANSFIELD • HŪRIA MĀTENGA • JEAN BATTEN
LISA KING • JANET FRAME • JOAN WIFFEN
LORDE • WHINA COOPER • KATE EDGER
LYDIA KO • MARGARET MAHY • JANET FRAM
MAI CHEN • KATE SHEPPARD • LISA TAMAT
KAREN WALKER • JEAN BATTEN • RITA ANGUS • MAVIS RIVER
LUCY LAWLESS • LUCY LAWLESS • MERATA MITA
MARGARET CRUIKSHANK • TE PUEA HERANGI • NANCY WAKE • NANCY WAKE
MOJO MATHERS • MERATA MITA • MIRA SZÁSZY
NEROLI FAIRHALL • GEORGINA BEYER • MICHELLE DICKINSON
RITA ANGUS • MARGARET MAHY
• PARRIS GOEBEL • PATRICIA GRACE
SELINA TUSITALA MARSH • RUIA MORRISON • SOPHIE PASCOE
SUZIE MONCRIEFF • TE PUEA HERANGI
SUZANNE AUBERT • VALERIE ADAMS • HELEN CLARK
WHINA COOPER • YVETTE WILLIAMS • KATE EDGER
BEATRICE FAUMUINA

Preface

Every girl can become a hero. She might stun the world; she might make only a few people proud and happy. She might keep her bravery to herself. True heroes just want to do their best at whatever it happens to be.

When the publisher asked me to write stories of successful New Zealand women, I never considered saying no. I wasn't sure I'd meet the challenge but I absolutely wanted to try because young people — actually, all of us — need real-life stories that encourage us to stay true to our own goals.

The first task was choosing who to include. We stopped the list at about 200 and could have added many more. The narrowing-down began. We had to find inspirational stories about a wide range of achievements.

None of the contemporary women in these pages knew we were working on *Go Girl.* When at last we told them, we hoped they'd realise their tales are here not only to say how amazing they are. Their stories were also chosen to show how girls became successful scientists, athletes, writers, lawyers, artists, social campaigners and more. You — the reader — can see each girl, in her own time, discovering the confidence and determination to be successful in her own way.

If you're seven years old, seventeen, or older than twenty-seven, these heroes are waiting for you to join them.

Barbara Else
August 2017

Ahumai Te Paerata

Warrior

c. 1824–1908 | Born in Waikato;
Ngāti Te Kohera and Ngāti Raukawa

KI TE MATE NGĀ TĀNE, ME MATE ANŌ NGĀ WĀHINE ME NGĀ TAMARIKI.

In the sad time of the New Zealand Wars, a young Māori woman, Ahumai, showed two kinds of extraordinary courage.

With only 300 others, she was trapped for three days in the Ōrākau Pā in the Waikato. Over 1500 British soldiers surrounded them. The battles had been long and hard, and it was clear the Māori could not win this one.

The British flew the white flag of truce. 'We admire your bravery,' shouted an officer. 'Let the fighting stop. Come out so you will be saved.'

'Peace shall be made never. Never, never!' rang the reply.

The officer shouted again. 'That is well for you men. But it is not right for the women and children. Send them out so they will be safe.'

There was silence while the chiefs considered.

But Ahumai stood up on the parapet of Ōrākau. Her brave voice filled the air: 'Ki te mate ngā tāne, me mate anō ngā wāhine me ngā tamariki.' ('If the men die, the women and children will die also.')

The British prepared to renew the fight.

But the Māori warriors came up with a final plan. When the British least expected it, they simply rushed out. They were chased on horseback, and the fighting was brutal.

Ahumai suffered dreadful bullet wounds. But she survived. So did her brother.

They lay hidden until night, then struggled away.

One year later, Ahumai had barely recovered from her wounds. The remnants of her tribe had become Hauhau, followers of a movement set on revenge. She was with them in a tiny village.

An English naval officer on his travels with a Māori guide came upon them. The chief Te Ao Katoa demanded that the young man be killed.

Ahumai herself had strong reason to want vengeance. But she said not a word. Slowly she stood and walked across to the young officer. Still silent, she faced the crowd, then sat beside him.

The warriors respected Ahumai's soundless declaration and set the English officer free.

Ahumai showed two kinds of bravery. One was the courage to stand with her people. The other was the courage to stand apart from them in order to show generosity.

ILLUSTRATED BY Helen Taylor

Beatrice Faumuina

Athlete

Born 1974 in Auckland, New Zealand

IF YOU SHARE YOUR DREAMS WITH PEOPLE YOU TRUST, IT HELPS YOU REACH YOUR GOAL. IT WORKS FOR SPORT AND WITH ANYTHING ELSE YOU DECIDE TO TRY.

Once a girl called Beatrice was born to Samoan parents in the sprawling city of Auckland. She was an only child. She loved swimming and gymnastics. She was good at athletics, softball and netball. It was fun playing in teams with other children.

When Bea was a teenager, she wondered if she'd be any good at shot put or discus. After all, she was big and strong. So she found coaches. Miriam had been a New Zealand throwing champion; Max was a champion, too.

Very soon, with their advice Beatrice herself was a champion. At 18 years old she set a new national discus record. She was so grateful to her coaches.

The next year, Beatrice won a silver medal at the Commonwealth Games.

Then sadly, Miriam died. Beatrice felt distraught without Miriam as her friend. She felt lost without Miriam's coaching.

Other friends consoled Bea and helped her find Les. He'd been a gold medallist, too, and was a weight-training expert.

'You're a great athlete, Bea,' he said, 'and you can be better than great. Work harder.'

Bea was also studying for a diploma in Business Studies. But she made time to train. Les encouraged her to keep sweating with heavier and heavier weights, building up strength.

Before long, Bea qualified for the World Championships in Athens.

And she won the gold medal for discus.

That year, Bea kept winning event after event. She was ranked number one in the world.

The next year she won gold at the Commonwealth Games.

And she kept winning. She became so famous that Samoa even put her image on a postage stamp.

Bea thought she'd better start figuring out what to do next, especially when it came time to stop competing. She worked for the United Nations. Later she was a TV presenter on the New Zealand programme *Tagata Pasifika*. But the main thing was that she finished her studies.

Eventually, she became head of the BEST Pasifika Leadership Academy. There, just as her coaches had done for her, Bea could encourage young Pasifika women and men to believe in themselves and push themselves harder. She says: If you share your dreams with people you trust, it helps you reach your goal. It works for sport and with anything else you decide to try.

ILLUSTRATED BY Fifi Colston

Beatrice Tinsley

Astronomer

1941–1981 | Born in England; immigrated to New Zealand in 1946

BY THE TIME SHE WAS 14, SHE KNEW THAT THE FIELD OF SCIENCE SHE LOVED BEST WAS ASTROPHYSICS – HOW STARS EVOLVE.

There was once a woman whose life was bound by ridiculous rules. Her name was Beatrice. She was a searcher, a putter-together of little things that added up to big ideas. By the time she was 14, she knew that the field of science she loved best was astrophysics — how stars evolve. In that science, she said, 'things always change!'

When she was at Canterbury University, Beatrice married another scientist. But they discovered a ridiculous rule: at that time, two married people could not both work in the same university.

They moved to Austin, Texas, where her husband had been offered a job at that university. They found the same ridiculous rule was in place there. For Beatrice it must have felt like a dark band across her sky.

But she studied hard, hopeful she would discover new things about stars and galaxies. By now they had adopted two children. Beatrice loved them, bright little stars in her own heart and home.

She gained her Doctor of Philosophy with a thesis about galaxies.

The examiners called her work 'extraordinary and profound'. The American Astronomical Society gave her their award for outstanding research and promise as a woman astronomer. She was discovering how stars and galaxies grew and died.

Beatrice helped design a new Department of Astronomy for the Texas university. Surely now they'd give her a full-time job? She wrote and applied to work in the new department.

Even after all that she had done, they had so little respect for her they didn't even reply.

Her heart was torn in two. Beatrice had so much to offer — but she couldn't work as a scientist in the place her family lived. She had to make a terrible choice. Whatever she did, many would say it was wrong. But Beatrice had been scorned too often.

She left her husband and children, the stars of her heart, to continue her research.

Beatrice wrote many scientific papers and became the first woman professor of astronomy at Yale University.

Now she has a mountain named after her. She has an asteroid named after her, too. She was a bright star herself. But without her children her heart must often have been as dark as the darkest night.

ILLUSTRATED BY Ali Teo

Dame Catherine Tizard

Governor-General

Born 1931 in Waharoa, New Zealand

'WHAT A PEST FOR YOU,' SAID CATH.
'I'M CHANGING THAT RULE.'

In the tiny Waikato town of Waharoa, baby Catherine was born. Her parents called her Cath for short — no messing about.

When Cath grew up, she went to Auckland to study zoology. Soon she married and had four children. Life was busy, but she managed with not much messing about. When the children were old enough, she went back to her studies.

She became a city councillor. That led to her being on a TV chat show. Viewers liked her don't-mess-about manner and the way she laughed.

There had never been a woman mayor in Auckland. But Cath thought she'd have a try. She was elected, and life became even busier. She loved it. She was elected mayor two more times.

Then Cath was asked if she'd be Governor-General. There had never been a woman Governor-General in New Zealand before.

What would I need to be, as Governor-General? Cath thought. *Cheerful and sensible. Yes, I can do that.* So the Queen appointed her.

When Cath moved into Government House, she walked into the dining room. At once a servant stopped setting the table and stood still.

'What's the matter?' Cath asked.

'Madam,' said the servant, 'the rule is that as soon as the Governor-General appears we have to stop work.'

'What a pest for you,' said Cath. 'I'm changing that rule.'

When people came to Government House to meet Cath, they all bowed.

'Do stop that,' Cath said.

'Madam,' whispered an aide, 'it's the rule to bow to the Governor-General.'

'I'm changing that, too,' said Cath. 'No New Zealander should have to bow to another.'

In 2002, Cath was made a Member of the Order of New Zealand. One man wrote objecting that a woman had been given such a high honour.

Cath laughed. 'He doesn't seem to remember that the highest position in the land is actually the Queen.'

If Cath thought something was idiotic she said so: *no messing about.*

ILLUSTRATED BY Sarah Laing

Elizabeth McCombs

First woman MP

1873–1935 | Born in Kaiapoi, New Zealand

'EQUAL PAY FOR WOMEN,' DEMANDED ELIZABETH. 'GIVE UNEMPLOYED WOMEN AND YOUNG PEOPLE THE SAME RIGHTS AS UNEMPLOYED MEN.'

Once upon a time in Kaiapoi, a girl called Elizabeth was born into a poor and clever family.

They loved her very much. But as she grew, her older sisters murmured. 'Do you think Elizabeth is a little lazy?' 'Hmm — we will not expect great things of her.'

Elizabeth merely thought her own thoughts. Elizabeth watched with her clear, calm eyes.

She saw women did not have the same rights as men. She heard about sad cases of orphans and neglected children. As soon as she was old enough, she joined the Canterbury Children's Aid Society and started to do something about it.

When Elizabeth married, she and her husband, James, had two children of their own and adopted two orphans. James shared Elizabeth's wish to fight poverty. He became the first President of the Labour Party and won a seat in Parliament.

Elizabeth grew more determined to help the poor and needy, in large ways and small. She was elected to the Christchurch City Council, to hospital boards and charities. She had to argue with men who wanted to stop her from improving conditions for nurses (for instance).

New Zealand had never yet had a woman Member of Parliament. Elizabeth became determined to be the first. In 1928 she tried but failed. In 1931 she tried and failed again.

Then James died. Elizabeth was desperately sad. But she was also still very determined. She stood for Parliament in James's place.

One of her opponents scoffed. 'The difficulties of this country are too great for women to grapple with!' he said.

And, just as her sisters hadn't expected great things of Elizabeth, nobody expected much now. James himself had won the seat by only 32 votes.

But when the count was in, Elizabeth had won by 2600 votes. A landslide.

She had become New Zealand's first woman Member of Parliament.

'Equal pay for women,' demanded Elizabeth. 'Give unemployed women and young people the same rights as unemployed men.' She also said women should be able to join the police force.

She showed that women were the equal of men.

And the girl called lazy by her sisters became the most-remembered person of her family.

ILLUSTRATED BY Phoebe Morris

Ella Williams

Surfer

Born 1995 in Whangamatā, New Zealand

SHE FOUND A SURFING POSTER.
ON IT SHE WROTE:
I WILL BE A WORLD SURFING CHAMPION.

On the beach of Whangamatā, white curves of waves roll onto a white curve of sand. Steadily they break and retreat, then roll in again. Those waves are perfect for surfing.

A little girl called Ella loved to paddle in the edge of the surf. She watched the board riders swoop and battle the force of the waves, then swim out to ride in again.

'Me, too,' the little girl said.

Her dad gave her a foam body-board. With her mum and her brother, he showed Ella how to manage the smaller waves. It felt just as exciting as Ella had imagined.

As she grew, Ella longed to swoop as far and be as strong and steady as the grown-up surfers.

She found a surfing poster. On it she wrote: *I will be a world surfing champion.* Then she pinned it on her bedroom wall.

'Okay, Ella,' said her dad, mum and brother. 'Let's get serious.'

They found the best board for her size and weight, and helped her to train. They showed her the best ways to stand on the board, and talked about the best way to breathe when she battled the waves. They made videos of her surfing. Later, she studied them and learned how to become better and better.

All the time the poster stayed on her wall. *I will be a world surfing champion.*

She was very fit. But she worked to stay fit and be even better, by running, doing yoga, and trying all kinds of exercise.

Then Ella began to enter competitions.

Sometimes the tide and waves didn't help her. Sometimes they did. Ella just did the best she could with each wave, and learned how to do better.

Ella began to win competitions in New Zealand.

'More!' Ella told herself. *I will be a world surfing champion.*

After more effort, at last she won the Women's World Junior Surf Championship.

Now Ella has won competitions all over the world. The waves keep coming. Sometimes they help, sometimes they don't. Ella just keeps swooping, riding and battling, making the surfboard dance on powerful waves.

ILLUSTRATED BY Sophie Watson

Farah Palmer

Rugby player

Born 1972 in Te Kūiti | Ngāti Waiora, Ngāti Maniopoto, Ngāti Mahuta ki te hauāuru and Waikato

JUST GIVE IT A GO.
ASPIRE TO WHATEVER
YOU CHOOSE.

There once was a girl called Farah who was brought up in the King Country town of Piopio.

Farah loved trying stuff out. Say something new, and she was in there. Tap dancing? She didn't know if she'd be much good, but she'd give it a go. A school choir? There was Farah. A play? For sure, that might be fun. She was into athletics, swimming and netball. She never gave up, and was always encouraging her friends and team mates to be the best they could be.

When Farah was ready to leave school, she heard about scholarships to study Physical Education at Otago University. It was a long way from Piopio. No one in Farah's family had ever been to university. Could she try?

She was nervous. But she gave it a go. There, she found friends and other people to support her. And studying sport was fun.

In Dunedin, for the first time, she saw a women's rugby team. Could she try that? She was fairly small for a rugby player. But Farah simply had to give it a go.

And what a great game it turned out to be for teamwork, women working together. In a very short time, Farah was made captain.

Only five years later she became captain of the Black Ferns, the New Zealand women's rugby team. Three times she led them to World Cup victory.

Farah was still studying hard at university. She did so well that the professor asked if she'd like to go on studying, for a higher and harder degree.

Say something new and Farah was in there. She began studying how sport can change society, and gained her PhD.

She was named International Women's Personality of the Year by the International Rugby Board. She was listed in the International Rugby Board Hall of Fame. But for Farah, her rugby success was about the other women, not about her. It was all teamwork.

As for her success with her studies — Farah did that on her own. She encourages other women and girls: *Just give it a go. Aspire to whatever you choose.*

ILLUSTRATED BY Sarah Wilkins

Frances Hodgkins

Painter

1869–1947 | Born in Dunedin, New Zealand

SHE KEPT TRAVELLING AND PAINTING, AND CALLED HERSELF 'TERRIBLY' AMBITIOUS.

Once upon a time in the beautiful city of Dunedin, baby Frances was born. Her father was a good painter, and he encouraged Frances and her older sister, Isabel, to paint, too.

Frances and Isabel showed plenty of talent. Frances's father and Isabel preferred to paint landscapes. Most often Frances painted people.

She went to art school, hoping to qualify as an art teacher and then earn her own living.

Isabel married and kept on painting. But Frances thought her sister's work didn't develop, change and improve. Frances made up her mind that nothing would stop her from developing her own art.

When she was 21 she started to show paintings in New Zealand galleries.

At last she had saved enough money to travel to London and study further. She painted in countries all over Europe, and met many other artists of all kinds.

Her first great success came when one of her watercolours was the first work by a New Zealander to be shown at London's Royal Academy of Arts. It was *Fatima*, a Moroccan woman swathed in beautiful robes.

Although she owned hardly anything except her painting equipment, Frances loved being independent. She kept travelling and painting, and called herself 'terribly' ambitious. She could not stop painting.

And her work did develop. It began to show less interest in the human figure and more in soft colour and light. It moved towards being abstract and modern.

Frances returned to New Zealand for a while, but then moved back to Europe — Spain, France and England.

She was there when World War Two broke out. By now she was 70 years old. Her health wasn't good, but she kept painting as hard as ever.

Just after the war she was able to travel to London for an honour desired by all artists — an exhibition of her life's work.

A few months later, Frances died.

Another of New Zealand's greatest painters, Colin McCahon, often visited the Dunedin Art Gallery when he was a boy. His favourite work was a painting by Frances called *Summer*. He felt it sang to him from the wall.

Her paintings still hang in galleries all over the world.

ILLUSTRATED BY Vasanti Unka

Georgina Beyer

Politician and trailblazer

Born 1957 in Wellington | Te Āti Awa, Ngāti Mutunga, Ngāti Raukawa, Ngāti Porou

HE LEARNED THAT, FOR INSTANCE, YOU MIGHT BE BORN MALE BUT INSIDE YOU FEEL AND THINK LIKE A WOMAN.

Once upon a time there was a boy. His parents named him George after his great-grandfather, who'd been in the magnificent Māori Battalion.

As George grew up, he felt that his parents and teachers didn't understand him. He didn't understand himself either. Something about life was uncomfortable, and he had no idea what it could be. The one time he felt right was when he put on a dress and went to a movie all by himself. Not a soul realised who he was.

George was a bright child, but he couldn't bear to stay at school or at home when he felt so unhappy. So he left the moment he could.

Finally, out in the world, George realised there were other people who felt as he did — uneasy and wrong being labelled either male or female. He learned that, for instance, you might be born male but inside you feel and think like a woman.

George felt a huge sense of relief. It was as if he'd been on a troubling journey. Here at last was home for the heart.

He tossed every last piece of his boys' clothing on a bonfire. The fantastic blaze burnt them to ashes.

Changing his name was easy.

Now Georgina could be who she really was. She launched herself into the world anew, lively and vigorous.

Georgina was beautiful, full of pizzazz. Wherever she went she wore the most stylish clothes, with her hair always glamorous. She was classy, witty and straightforward. She was strong and fair.

She moved to the town of Carterton and worked on the radio.

She became a trailblazer — she was the first person in all the world who had switched from male to female to be elected the mayor of a town.

And there was more. Georgina stood for Parliament, as the Labour Party candidate for Wairarapa. Political experts said she'd never win.

But she did, with the most votes by far.

Georgina stood again at the next election and won by twice as many votes as she had before.

Trailblazer. Classy. Burning bright.

ILLUSTRATED BY Rebecca ter Borg

Hayley Westenra

Singer

Born 1987 in Christchurch, New Zealand

IMAGINE. YOU THINK YOU'RE AN ORDINARY GIRL IN AN ORDINARY FAMILY IN AN ORDINARY TOWN. BUT FAIRY TALES ARE KNOWN TO COME TRUE.

Imagine you're six years old. You're an ordinary girl in an ordinary family in an ordinary city.

Then imagine a teacher gives you a part in the school Christmas play. It's the lead role of 'Little Star'. It is scary. But you love singing.

Imagine someone hears you. She tells your parents: 'That child has perfect pitch. She ought to learn a musical instrument.'

So you learn to play the recorder and read music. You learn piano, violin and guitar.

Then imagine you're 12. You cut a demo album for your family and friends. It's great fun.

Imagine more fun, busking in the streets of Christchurch where you live.

Now imagine someone from TV walks by. 'Come and appear on air,' she says.

Soon a local recording company offers you a deal. You release a couple of CDs and become pretty well-known in New Zealand.

Now imagine — a big British record company wants to sign you up. It's scary. You're only 14. But you've been performing for eight years now. It's been great fun, but actually has been hard work, too. And you believe in your voice.

You record a CD of songs, a mixture of classical, traditional Māori and light pop. It's called *Pure*.

In the first week it's released, *Pure* reaches number eight in the US pop charts. It's number one in Britain.

Can you believe it?

Well, it happened to Hayley.

Now Hayley has recorded many albums and performed all over the world. She has sung before the Queen. On stage she has worn more beautiful dresses than she can probably remember.

It's like a fairy tale.

Imagine. You think you're an ordinary girl in an ordinary family in an ordinary town. But fairy tales are known to come true.

An ordinary town might have special opportunities hidden somewhere. An ordinary family might just have to discover that they're extraordinary. An ordinary girl just has to discover what makes her remarkable.

ILLUSTRATED BY Helen Taylor

Helen Clark

Prime Minister

Born 1950 in Te Pahu, New Zealand

'YOU CAN TAKE ME ON,' SHE SAID ONCE, 'BUT DON'T TRY TO INTIMIDATE ME.'

Near magical Mount Pirongia in the Waikato lies the settlement of Te Pahu. There on a farm, Helen lived with her three sisters. She worked hard feeding the chickens and milking the cows. She climbed in the orchard and played with the lambs.

Helen could read before she went to primary school, and she did well there. She loved Te Pahu.

It was a long way from the farm when she went boarding at secondary school in Auckland. But being in a city made Helen think about all sorts of things beyond chickens, lambs and the orchard.

And later, at university, Helen started to question: *Who should hold power in a country? How could that power be used to improve life for all of the people?*

She took part in protest marches and demonstrations. 'No foreign military bases in New Zealand!' shouted Helen. 'No Vietnam War!' she cried. 'No racism!'

Before too long Helen became a Member of Parliament. The first thing she did in the Debating Chamber was stand and say, 'It is wrong for the USA to have nuclear cruise missiles in the Pacific Ocean.'

Before too much longer, Helen became Minister of Health. This meant a new office, where someone had left behind an ordinary cheap black briefcase.

'Don't chuck it out,' Helen said. 'I'm going to use it.'

'But it's old,' said her secretary. 'You're a minister now. You need a new—'

'No, I don't. That one's right for the job,' Helen said. She filled it with the important papers she had to read and cart around.

At last Helen became the first New Zealand woman to lead her party to election victory. The briefcase was battered, but she still used it even though she was Prime Minister.

Helen won two more elections and stayed Prime Minister for nine years. In 2006, she ranked as the twentieth most powerful woman in the world.

Was she ever nervous?

'You can take me on,' she said once, 'but don't try to intimidate me.'

She kept the plain black briefcase for nearly 20 years, until it fell apart. It had been just right for her to get on with the job.

ILLUSTRATED BY Vasanti Unka

Hūria Mātenga

Shipwreck hero

c. 1840–1909 | Born in Whakapuaka;
Te Āti Awa, Ngāti Tama and Ngāti Toa

HŪRIA WANTED TO SWIM OUT AND SAVE HIM TOO – BUT EVEN AS SHE STARTED TO MOVE, THE WAVES TOOK HIM.

A baby girl, Ngarongoa Katene, was born near Nelson at Whakapuaka.

When she grew, she took the name of Hūria. She married Hemi Mātenga, a man as tall and strong as she was strong and beautiful.

One night there was a terrible storm. In the early morning, Hūria, Hemi and two other Māori men saw huge waves pounding over the sailing ship *Delaware*, which was wrecked on the rocks.

The ship's mate took a safety line and tried to swim it to shore. But a wave threw him against a boulder. He was dragged back aboard, but the crew thought he was dead.

Hūria and her companions rushed along the beach to try to help.

A second of the crew heaved another line overboard. Hūria and two of her group swam out for it.

After an age of struggle, Hūria was close enough to grasp the rope. She helped haul it onto the shore.

The rescuers fixed the rope around a huge boulder to pull it tight between the beach and the *Delaware*.

Now one by one each crewman plunged into the waves, then gripped the rope so he could labour towards the beach. The sea thrashed over the rope and tried to drag it away. The two strongest Māori held it as steady as possible.

Hūria was covered in bruises, cut by the rocks. But time after time, when a sailor managed to reach the breaking surf, she dived back in to guide him through. Then he could rest by a fire set burning on the beach by the fourth rescuer.

The sea raged on. The safety line began to rub through on the rock. As the captain, last to leave his ship, reached the shore, the line finally snapped.

It was then the first mate appeared, alive after all, on the deck of the *Delaware*.

Hūria wanted to swim out and save him, too — but even as she started to move, the waves took him.

The people of Nelson praised Hūria and her companions, and rewarded them.

Several artists painted the portrait of this strong woman. One still hangs in Nelson's Art Gallery. It recognises how with her brave deeds Hūria risked her own life.

ILLUSTRATED BY Phoebe Morris

Ingrid Visser

Marine biologist

Born 1966 in Lower Hutt, New Zealand

PROTECT THE ORCA AND WE ALSO PROTECT OUR BEAUTIFUL OCEAN.

Once upon a time, a little girl called Ingrid was born in Lower Hutt. She loved living close to the sea. She especially loved dolphins. Could she ever work with the largest of the dolphin family, the orca?

'The only place you can do that is somewhere like SeaWorld,' people said.

Orca in captivity? Even when she was a child, that didn't seem right to Ingrid.

For a while the family lived on a farm near the sea. Ingrid loved it. Then they moved inland to a bigger farm. She missed the ocean so much it hurt.

They moved again, nearer the ocean. Then, when she was 16, her father said, 'We're sailing a yacht around the world.'

Magical!

The ocean became as familiar to her as the land. Ingrid watched seabirds soar and dive for fish. She saw storms lash the waves. She saw dolphins and whales play in the ever-changing water. But never did she see orca up close.

When they'd sailed home, Ingrid studied zoology, to learn about animal behaviour and the creatures of the sea.

One day near the university marine station, a colleague shouted, 'Orca! Orca out there!'

As fast as she could, Ingrid pulled on her diving mask, snorkel and fins, and slipped into the water. A female orca approached and eyed her. Then it fetched its calf. The baby circled Ingrid faster and faster, so she felt she was in the middle of a magical game.

Ingrid began a project to get to know orca better, to film them and swim with them.

'Don't do it! They're dangerous,' people told her.

'Rubbish,' said Ingrid. 'There's never been a proven account of an orca attacking a human in the ocean. Only in captivity.'

And she couldn't bear the idea of orca trapped in a concrete tank, performing tricks in front of an audience.

She found there were fewer than 200 orca around New Zealand. Now they come to Ingrid for a scratch, to show off and play. She analyses what they eat — sharks and rays — to see what kind of chemicals enter the sea and poison its creatures. 'Protect the orca and we also protect our beautiful ocean,' Ingrid says.

ILLUSTRATED BY Fifi Colston

Dame Jane Campion

Film director

Born 1954 in Wellington, New Zealand

THE PLACE YOU GROW UP HELPS TO FORM YOUR IMAGINATION.

Once, a girl called Jane grew up in Wellington. She and her older sister lived in a world full of imagination. Their mother was an actor. Their father was a theatre and opera director. People assumed Jane would grow up and work in the theatre, too.

Instead, she studied anthropology, all about human beings. Then she went to London to study art.

Finally, Jane studied at film school. Didn't movie-making combine anthropology, art and theatre?

With her first short film, she won the Palme d'Or at the Cannes Film Festival.

Soon Jane made a feature film called *Sweetie*. Some people thought it was weird. But if some people didn't like *weird*, plenty more did. *Sweetie* won awards, too.

Jane's next movie was *An Angel at My Table*, about the famous New Zealand writer, Janet Frame. People began to take more notice of Jane now: *Where is she from? New Zealand? Hmm, a director to watch.*

Her next movie, *The Piano*, shot Jane to the top ranks of film-makers. The actor who played the main character won the Oscar for Best Actress. The girl who played the woman's daughter won Best Supporting Actress. None of that happens without a great director.

Jane herself won an Academy Award for Best Original Screenplay. It's not easy to write a screenplay and be the director as well.

And she was the first woman ever to win the Palme d'Or for a full-length film.

The Piano has become a classic. It's a masterpiece.

Since then, Jane's made other movies and TV series. Her characters are often women who find it hard to speak out. They struggle and strive for inner confidence about their place in the world. They're dogged and tough, extraordinary women.

Jane lives overseas most of the time now. But she loves to come home to New Zealand as often as she can. She says, 'The place you grow up helps to form your imagination.'

ILLUSTRATED BY Sarah Laing

Janet Frame

Writer

1924–2004 | Born in Dunedin, New Zealand

WHAT SHE NEEDED WAS TO WRITE STORIES THAT SHOWED THE BEAUTY, JOY AND HEARTACHE OF OUR ORDINARY WORLD.

Once there was a girl called Janet who loved stories and poems. With her sisters and brother and friends, she was always acting out stories. She grew dizzy with delight when she was given her own notebook to fill with her own words.

She won school prizes. One prize was a book, *Boys and Girls who Became Famous*.

Janet dreamed of fame. In her diary she wrote that her family expected her to be a teacher. But she was determined to be a poet.

Terrible news came one day when she was 12: her oldest sister had drowned. There's no comfort for such a tragedy. But Janet read the words of great poets and felt they understood how much she grieved.

She began teacher training, but in the end she said 'Excuse me' and simply walked out. What she needed was to write stories that showed the beauty, joy and heartache of our ordinary world.

Gradually Janet found the courage to show her writing to people she trusted. A publisher called the stories 'extraordinary'. He promised he'd bring them out as a book.

In the same month, a second sister of Janet's died of drowning. The burden of sorrow overwhelmed any happiness about her stories.

And it took years for the book *The Lagoon and Other Stories* to be published. Meanwhile, doctors said Janet was so ill that they intended to operate on her brain. But *The Lagoon and Other Stories* won a prize for best book of prose that year, and the doctors decided not to meddle with her brilliant mind.

Other writers and book-lovers helped Janet by giving her a place to write. She worked on her first novel, *Owls do Cry*, based on her own ordinary yet also remarkable childhood.

In New Zealand and around the world, Janet began to win more and more writing awards.

But fame can mean other people constantly demand too much of you. Janet politely refused many invitations to be interviewed or speak in front of an audience. She was happier being mischievous with family and friends. She was at her absolute happiest when she was writing. Writing, writing.

ILLUSTRATED BY Sarah Wilkins

AN ANGEL
MY TABLE
THE WATER
ISLAND

Jean Batten

Aviator

1909–1982 | Born in Rotorua, New Zealand

JEAN WAS 18 WHEN SHE RESOLVED TO BE A FAMOUS FLIER.

Jean was 18 when she resolved to be a famous flier. It took years and lots of hard work. Finally, she felt ready to break Amy Johnson's record of 18 days for a woman's solo flight from England to Australia.

In a brown paper parcel, Jean wrapped her red lipstick and a white satin frock. She checked the spare fuel tank, safe in the front seat of her Gipsy Moth plane, and the spare propeller, which was strapped tight between the two cockpits. Then she climbed into the cramped rear seat — the pilot seat.

From England to Italy, the engine purred. Jean nibbled a chicken leg. On the next stage, to Syria, she was cold, although she enjoyed the danger.

On the third stage, to Karachi in Pakistan, a sandstorm darkened the sky. The plane's instruments were almost useless. Jean nearly crashed, but managed to land in the desert.

She set off when the storm was over. But almost at once wind and sand whipped the plane again.

Jean flew above it, and found night was falling. She had to land again. The ground was bumpy with rocks, but she held the plane steady until it came to rest.

Bruised and aching, with her face bleeding from the lash of sand grains, Jean climbed out of her plane to find water. In the dark she fell over the corpse of a camel and ran from a giant land crab. She was so tired, she simply pulled cushions out of the plane and fell asleep on the ground.

When she woke, eight Arab men were staring at her and the plane in astonishment. She swung the propeller, leapt into the cockpit and took off.

Yet another sandstorm tossed Jean around and forced her to land. This time the propeller was cracked. The spare propeller had vanished.

Villagers from nearby helped her with repairs, then Jean took to the air once more.

But close to Karachi the engine broke. She tried to glide the plane so it could land on a highway, but the wings hit road-marker blocks and the plane flipped over.

Jean struggled out. Her dream of flying solo to Australia this time was dashed. She knew she'd try again and succeed —

Then she saw a vulture circling above.

But the dust plume of a car was speeding towards her.

'It's my unlucky day,' she shouted up at the vulture. 'But — guess what?— it's yours, too!'

ILLUSTRATED BY Ali Teo

LONDON
EUROPE
BRINDISI
ATHENS
CYPRUS
AFRICA
OCEAN
KOEPANG
PT. DARWIN
AUSTRALIA
SYDNEY
NEW PLYMOUTH

Joan Wiffen

Palaeontologist

1922–2009 | Born in Hawke's Bay, New Zealand

IN HER HAND, JOAN FELT THE WEIGHT OF AN ANCIENT GIFT OF NATURE. SHE LONGED TO FIND MORE FOR HERSELF.

Joan's father didn't believe women needed an education. They should just marry and have a family. So Joan had to leave school when she turned 16.

She served six years in the Women's Auxiliary Air Force.

When she did marry, Joan enjoyed family trips to the beach or into the hills of Hawke's Bay, to collect rocks.

Then one day someone gave her an ammonite, a fossilised, coiled sea creature that had been buried for millions of years. In her hand, Joan felt the weight of an ancient gift of Nature. She longed to find more for herself.

Joan may not have had much education, but she had intelligence. She decided to study fossils, which is known as palaeontology. So she taught herself to recognise the fossils of leaves and insects, and to use chisels and acid to get them out of the stone.

One day she noticed tiny writing on a map of the Te Hoe Valley: *reptilian bones in brackish water*. Could it be dinosaurs? Joan couldn't wait to go and see. She had no idea that scientists thought New Zealand couldn't have any dinosaur fossils.

The valley was rugged, the stream swift. So many fossils of the ordinary sort lay about that Joan grew more excited. She was sure that somewhere out there lay ancient treasure. But she found nothing out of the ordinary.

The next day, again she found nothing unusual except the great number of fossils. But Joan and her family returned time after time, month after month.

At last they struggled across a new part of the stream and began climbing higher up the valley.

There in the stream was a grey boulder. And in the boulder showed — *black reptilian bones*.

Joan had to work for years to prove it was a dinosaur. She had to teach herself more and more, but she persevered. Finally, it was certain: Joan, self-taught palaeontologist, had discovered the tailbone of a therapod, the first dinosaur fossil ever found in New Zealand.

She found more dinosaur fossils: fragments of mosasaur skulls, the toe bone of a therapod, bones of a pterosaur.

Trained scientists were amazed, and delighted, too.

Massey University made Joan, who had to leave school when she was 16, an Honorary Doctor of Science for her self-taught skill and her discoveries.

ILLUSTRATED BY Phoebe Morris

Karen Walker

Fashion designer

Born 1969 in Auckland, New Zealand

THERE WERE LITTLE TRIUMPHS AND LITTLE FAILURES. BUT KAREN KEPT ON GOING UNTIL SHE HAD MORE TRIUMPHS THAN FAILURES.

Once upon a time in Auckland, a young girl called Karen showed her Barbie doll to her grandmother.

'Do you want us to make Barbie a skirt?' Grandmother asked.

'Please!' said Karen.

So Grandmother cut out a square of fabric. She folded it into a triangle, then twice more, to make a smaller triangle each time. Then she folded it a fourth time to make a skinny triangle. 'Look at both sides,' Grandmother said. 'See that extra end piece? Take the scissors and snip it off.'

Karen's seven-year-old hands managed nicely.

She opened the fabric. Like magic, the square had turned into a circle.

'Fold it all back again,' Grandmother said. 'Now snip off the point at the top. Good.'

By now Karen realised how it worked. She cut once more up the circle to the hole in the middle, so that the fabric would wrap around Barbie. Grandmother showed her how to sew a ribbon for tying it on.

Karen was in love with sewing now. She taught herself to make other clothes. She went on to Epsom Girls' Grammar, but could hardly wait to finish school and begin fashion college.

'Can you make me a shirt?' a friend asked.

'I'm up for that,' Karen replied.

Other people liked the shirt and asked for one, too.

This is how Karen started a career as a fashion designer. For the first five years, she did it all herself. She thought up the designs. She cut the fabric and sewed it. She swept up the scraps. She sent out bills to get paid for the clothing she made.

She wanted her clothes to be easy to wear, and also different from those of other designers. There were little triumphs and little failures. But Karen kept on going until she had more triumphs than failures.

Finally, she had five of her own stores in New Zealand. Karen had to work harder to keep the fashion ideas coming. Her clothes had started selling all over the world. Famous stars like Madonna wore her designs.

And it started with a Barbie, Grandmother, a square of fabric and a seven-year-old girl who thought: *I'm up for this*.

ILLUSTRATED BY Sarah Laing

Kate Edger

Scholar

1857–1935 | Born in England; immigrated to New Zealand in 1862

SHE WAS ALSO PRESENTED WITH A WHITE CAMELLIA, A SIGN OF HER 'UNPRETENDING EXCELLENCE' – WHICH PROBABLY MEANT SHE MADE NO FUSS ABOUT BEING SO CLEVER.

She was small and quiet with her eyes downcast. She was Kate Edger, the first girl to attend Auckland College and Grammar School.

In two other New Zealand cities and other parts of the world, girls already had their own secondary schools. But it hadn't happened yet in Auckland in the 1870s. Many people worried that too much education would harm a woman's brain.

But Kate's father and mother wanted good teaching for their clever child, so they persuaded the headmaster to accept Kate into the boys' school. He found she was so intelligent that he placed her in the top class.

But he told her to keep her eyes down and stay quiet.

Kate was determined to keep studying after secondary school. But it was the same situation — in other parts of the world and even New Zealand, women were attending university, but not in Auckland in the 1870s.

She wrote to the chancellor of the university, gave her school marks and applied for a scholarship. She left out the fact that she was a girl.

If the chancellor knew Kate wasn't a boy, he didn't want any fuss. He accepted her application.

Kate might have been small and quiet, but no one could doubt her determination. She became the first woman in New Zealand — in fact the first woman in the British Empire — to gain the degree of Bachelor of Arts. She was also presented with a white camellia, a sign of her 'unpretending excellence' — which probably meant she made no fuss about being so clever.

Kate became the first principal of Nelson College for Girls.

The headmaster of the Nelson boys' school muttered, 'Hrmph, a school for girls? That's not likely to last. Too many people believe the most noble area for women to work is in the home.'

But in its very first year, Nelson Girls ended up with more pupils than the boys' school.

Kate did a lot of the teaching herself: English grammar, literature, science, mathematics, Latin, geography and singing.

'Louder,' Kate cried. 'Sing your hearts out!'

She also taught exercise drills and club swinging.

'Swing those clubs!' shouted Kate. 'Stand tall, girls — and keep your eyes up!'

Kate Sheppard

Suffragist

1847–1934 | Born in England; immigrated to New Zealand in 1869

'WE RELY ON OUR HUSBANDS TO CHOOSE THE POLITICIANS FOR US.' KATE SMILED POLITELY AND THOUGHT 'RUBBISH'.

EQUALITY

Far away in England lived little Kate. When she was 16, her father died. She had an older sister already living in Christchurch. So her mother brought Kate, another sister and two brothers on the long, dangerous voyage by sailing ship to New Zealand.

Kate had a good education for a woman in those days, and loved to argue for justice. She thought alcohol made men neglect their wives and children, and caused poverty and illness. So she joined the Women's Christian Temperance Union to campaign against it. Kate was a good and intelligent speaker. She needed to be — the Temperance Union got into dozens of arguments.

People believed women were too fragile to ride bicycles. But Kate joined the first all-women cycling club in Christchurch. 'Outrageous!' the stuffy ones cried.

She decided tight corsets and long skirts weren't sensible, and went riding in knickerbockers, with no corset at all. 'Shocking!' the stuffy ones cried even louder.

'It would be unwomanly for women to vote in elections!' roared many men. Some women agreed: 'We rely on our husbands to choose the politicians for us.'

Kate smiled politely and thought *Rubbish*.

In 1888, with wit and common-sense she wrote: Ten reasons why the women of New Zealand should vote. She organised three petitions about it to Parliament. The first was in 1891. It had no effect. The next was in 1892. Still no effect.

Then in 1893 nearly 32,000 women and men signed a third petition. There were 547 sheets of signatures.

Kate glued all of the pages together. She wound them up around a broom-handle and sent it to Parliament. It was carried into the Debating Chamber and tossed so that it unrolled down the long central aisle — it hit the end wall with a thud.

That very year New Zealand became the first country in the world where all women could vote.

Kate kept arguing to make life better for women and children. During her lifetime, the newspapers often printed letters and articles both for her and against.

But when she died, the *Christchurch Times* said, 'A great woman has gone.'

ILLUSTRATED BY Sophie Watson

EQUALITY

Katherine Mansfield

(Kathleen Mansfield Beauchamp)

Writer

1888–1923 | Born in Wellington, New Zealand

SHE WAS DETERMINED TO SHOW WHAT LIFE WAS REALLY LIKE UNDER THE SURFACE, IN THE HEARTS AND THOUGHTS OF REAL PEOPLE.

Once a little girl was born in Wellington. Her name was Kathleen Mansfield Beauchamp. Compared to the families in the workers' cottages just down the road, her family was very well-off.

When Kathleen turned 16, her parents sent her to school in London. After three years she had to come home. She didn't want to. Her parents insisted.

With her bright brown eyes, Kathleen observed New Zealand afresh. By now her father was making even more money. But often, she saw, the rich didn't consider how the poor people felt.

It was now she decided to become a serious writer. When some of her pieces were accepted, she decided the name she would put on them would be 'Katherine Mansfield'. She didn't bother — or dare — to tell her parents. Her family bored her. How they annoyed her!

Her father decided she was being difficult, and so would let her return to England. But first, he sent her on a trip around central New Zealand. She admired the Māori she met there, and saw how deeply their hearts were connected to the land. Her need to write grew more powerful.

At last Katherine was in England again. It wasn't easy for a young woman on her own to fit in. But she managed.

Katherine married. On the very day of the wedding, she and her husband were having dinner when she thought, *Good grief, this whole thing is not for me.* And she walked out.

Her second marriage was to a magazine editor. Sometimes Katherine was not very well. But her stories kept flowing. She was determined to show what life was really like under the surface, in the hearts and thoughts of real people. Other great writers admired her work and encouraged her.

Then Katherine learned she had tuberculosis, a disease of the lungs. She tried all sorts of cures. Nothing helped.

In her last months she hardly wrote at all. But she was too young to die — her mind was aglow with a new way of seeing life and literature. She was impatient to recover, to set it all down . . .

She died without writing any more.

But Katherine's short stories still make her one of the world's most famous writers.

ILLUSTRATED BY Fifi Colston

Lisa King

Social entrepreneur

Born 1977 | Kiwi Chinese;
immigrated to New Zealand in 1980

*EVERYONE NEEDS LUNCH!
COULD SHE START SOMETHING
THAT MIGHT GROW, AND
HELP KIDS TO GROW?*

Once upon a time a very short while ago, right in Auckland city, there was a mother of two children. Her name was Lisa.

All week Lisa worked for a big company. It sold all kinds of things — junk food, soft drinks, chocolates and bags of chippies.

One day she saw an item on a TV news programme about lunchboxes in Auckland schools. Many children had very little in their lunchboxes. Some had nothing at all.

Lisa was shocked. She had heard about child poverty, and families who couldn't afford to give their children three meals a day. But the *Campbell Live* programme showed proof directly in front of her.

In this beautiful city of Auckland, and other beautiful cities and towns all over New Zealand, children were hungry. Hungry kids can't learn properly. They can't even play with much energy. Families might be embarrassed to send their children to school if they had no food, so the children might not go to school at all. Children worrying if they'd be fed or not would be unhappy.

Lots of people were talking about the problem. But who was doing anything?

A fire began burning in Lisa. A few free lunches couldn't help this huge problem. It was impossible to fix the problem everywhere right away. But everyone needs lunch! Could she start something that might grow, and help kids to grow?

Lisa thought about her job. She didn't let her own kids eat junk food. So why was she selling it? But in order to feed her own kids, Lisa needed a job.

Soon Lisa figured out a way for her to have work that also helped hungry kids.

She found a business partner. She found a great chef.

'Who needs lunch?' she asked them.

'Everyone does,' they said.

'Right,' said Lisa. 'So we're going to make healthy lunches for people too busy to make their own. For each lunch we sell, we give another healthy one to a kid who needs it. Everyone who buys a lunch helps a hungry kid. Win-win.'

'How soon can we start?' asked the business partner and chef.

Lisa called the new business Eat My Lunch. It started small. It's getting bigger, making thousands of kids happier and healthier. Everyone needs lunch.

ILLUSTRATED BY Ali Teo

Some
Kid
ate my
lunch
eat my lunch

Lisa Tamati

Runner

Born 1968 in New Plymouth |
Te Āti Awa and Ngāti Raukawa

OH REALLY? THOUGHT LISA.
SHE DECIDED TO SEE
FOR HERSELF.

Once a doctor in New Plymouth told a girl called Lisa she had such bad asthma that she could never play sport.

Oh really? thought Lisa. She decided to see for herself. Soon she was running and cycling, just for fun.

When she was 21, she broke her back in a flying-fox accident. The doctors said she'd never play sport again. They wanted to operate and fuse two of the bones in her spine.

Oh really?

Lisa said no. She decided to get better by doing core exercises to strengthen her back.

She pushed herself hard. Soon she was running and cycling again. But heading around and around a track grew too boring. She decided to push herself harder.

She went on cycle trips in different countries. She went climbing and trekking. Her boyfriend was with her, and he pushed her, too. At first this was okay. On their adventures Lisa found she could cycle and trek much further than she'd imagined.

Then they began to trek through the Libyan Desert. The heat was intense. This was harder than hard. At last Lisa's boyfriend told her she was hopeless.

Oh really? Lisa thought. She set off without him.

She made it across the desert. It had been so hard that Lisa took months to recover properly. But she had done it.

Next, Lisa ran across the Moroccan Sahara Desert.

She wanted to run the Badwater Ultramarathon. It's the hardest ultra-marathon, through Death Valley, the hottest place on the planet. There, if you break an egg on a stone it fries in seconds. Before she went, Lisa had some medical tests. She was told she had a below-average lung capacity and no talent for endurance running.

Oh really. Lisa shrugged. She ran Badwater anyway.

Back in New Zealand, Lisa ran the length of the country to raise money for charity.

She has proved she's a runner. She's kept on running ultra-marathons up mountains and over deserts. She's been named Māori Sportswoman of the Year. But she keeps searching out new challenges to beat, just to see for herself whether she can.

ILLUSTRATED BY Sarah Wilkins

Lorde

(Ella Yelich-O'Connor)

Singer

Born 1996 in Auckland, New Zealand

LYRICS AND MUSIC BEGAN POURING OUT OF HER. SHE WROTE ABOUT BEING YOUNG WITH HER FRIENDS, HOW IT FELT AND WHAT IT MEANT.

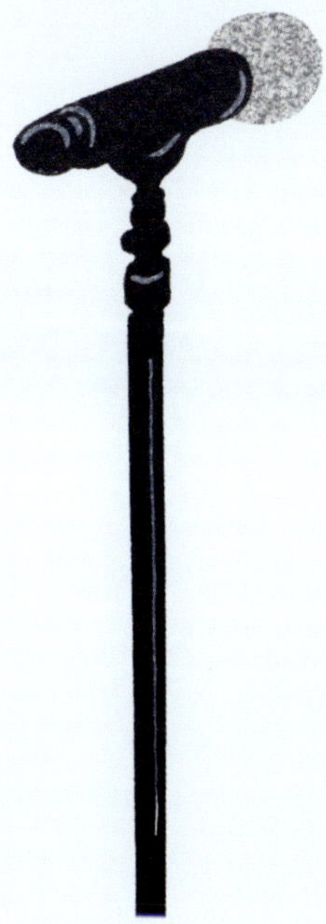

Once there was a girl who didn't plan to be a singer. Her name was Ella, and she lived in Auckland. She loved drama lessons and reading.

Ella read so many books that she was chosen for Kids' Lit Quiz, and her team came runner-up in the world finals. By now Ella was sure she'd be a writer.

But things don't always turn out how you think.

At intermediate school, Ella and a friend sang and played in the talent quest. They won. Then they were asked to sing on afternoon radio. Next thing, Ella was signed up for development with Universal Music Group.

For development? thought Ella. *Okay, I guess it means singing lessons*.

She listened to jazz and soul music. She played CDs of Fleetwood Mac, and far too many other great groups and musicians to say in a hundred breaths.

She co-wrote songs with her friend Joel. She tried writing her own songs, too, but somehow they didn't make her feel satisfied.

At last it was time to record an EP, and Ella had to find a stage name. Lord — with an 'e' — she decided. Lorde.

On free download, Lorde released *The Love Club*, four songs she co-wrote with Joel. One of them was called 'Royals'. It was about being happy and ordinary, not envious of the super-rich and super-famous, about loving just being with your friends. The EP had 60,000 hits.

Then Universal Music Group released it for sale.

Three months later, Universal released 'Royals' on its own. Sales went crazy.

Lorde, only 16 years old, had a number-one hit. The song expressed something in the hearts of young people all over the world.

Ella kept trying to write her own songs. They still didn't work for her. Then she read some short stories and something clicked. Finally she understood how to make words say what she wanted.

Lyrics and music began pouring out of her. She wrote about being young with her friends, how it felt and what it meant. Her words, her voice and her music came together.

Things didn't turn out how Ella expected. They turned out better. She's a singer, and a writer — a writer of songs.

ILLUSTRATED BY Rebecca ter Borg

Lucy Lawless

Actor and activist

Born 1968 in Auckland, New Zealand

BUT IN THE REAL WORLD, LUCY FIGHTS, TOO.

Her name is Lucy. She's tall and strong and fights for Good. She has millions of fans.

Lucy grew up in a sprawling, boisterous family. When she was 10, she took part in a school musical, and she was hooked. Through secondary school she kept acting and singing. She was pretty good.

After that, she had small parts here and there on TV, studied drama in Canada, then returned home.

A TV series called *Hercules: The Legendary Journeys* was being made in New Zealand, and Lucy played another couple of small parts. Everyone thought, *Yes, she's pretty good*.

In a later episode, she played Xena, an Amazon who was a villain. Everyone thought, *Wow, she's really good!*

'The fans love her,' said the TV writers. 'Let's turn that character into a hero. We'll have a new series about Xena the Warrior Princess, tall and strong, fighting for Good.'

Xena: Warrior Princess was a massive hit all over the world.

Lucy has taken many other roles, singing and acting in film and TV, fighting for good or evil or in-between.

But in the real world, Lucy fights, too.

She believes in saving the planet for her children and grandchildren. She doesn't just say so. Lucy takes action. For instance . . .

A rig was about to set off to Antarctica to look for oil. Greenpeace wanted to stop it, so Lucy and six other activists boarded the rig, climbed it as high as they could, and lashed themselves on.

Because of her fame as Xena, the whole world heard about the protest, and had to think about how using oil was bad for the climate and the world's future.

It took four days before Lucy and the others were brought down.

She was arrested, charged with burglary and put in jail. The judge fined her and the other protestors (although not very much).

Did Lucy care? Not at all. She said her victory as herself was more important than any of Xena's, the Warrior Princess.

ILLUSTRATED BY Sophie Watson

Lydia Ko

Golfer

Born 1997 in South Korea;
immigrated to New Zealand in 2003

*LYDIA BECAME BETTER
AT GOLF, AND BETTER.*

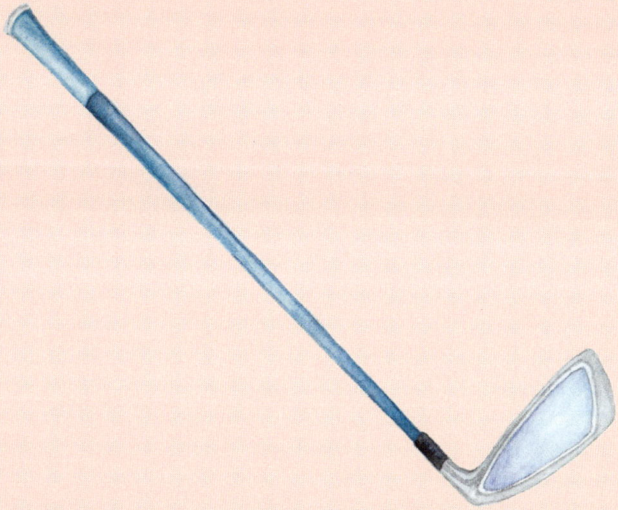

Once, far away in Korea, baby Bo-Gyung was born. The happy little girl loved being busy.

When she was five, she went with her mother to visit her aunt. The aunt played golf. The little girl had never seen this game before, and she was curious.

'Have a try,' said her aunt, and gave her a ball and two adult-sized clubs.

Little Bo-Gyung kept her eye on the ball and hit it each time. (Well, nearly. After all, she was only five.)

'That's pretty good,' her aunt said. 'Let's go and have the clubs cut down to your size.'

Bo-Gyung handled the shortened clubs very well indeed.

Back home again, her mother took her to an indoor golf course. The little girl grew better and better at hitting the balls.

Then the family moved to New Zealand, and Bo-Gyung became Lydia. She loved the wide, blue sky. She loved the beaches of Auckland's North Shore. She enjoyed going to school and laughing with her new friends.

And Lydia absolutely loved playing golf outside.

When she was seven, Lydia competed in the New Zealand Women's Amateur Championships. She didn't know the rules too well yet (after all, how old was she?), but people liked seeing her skip down the fairways. And she could certainly hit those balls.

Lydia became better at golf, and better. She began winning match after match, and travelled to overseas tournaments, where she won as well.

She had to keep up with her schoolwork, too. That became harder with each year. Often she had to learn by correspondence when she'd rather be out laughing with friends. She missed being a normal teenager. But she kept calm under the pressure of so many grown-ups around her and the tension of tournaments.

And she kept laughing. Lydia's personality made her so popular with journalists that she had to start saying no to requests for interviews. She might have natural talent, but she still had to keep up her golf practice.

Such a level-headed kid, shouted the journalists.

Lydia laughed and kept her eye on the ball.

ILLUSTRATED BY Helen Taylor

Mai Chen

Lawyer

Born 1963 in Taiwan;
immigrated to New Zealand in 1970

BUT MAI MADE A DECISION. SHE WOULD MAKE HER MARK ON NEW ZEALAND.

Once upon a time Mai Chen was born in Taiwan. Her parents already had three daughters and wanted a son. Very early on, Mai knew she had to prove that a fourth girl was as good as a boy.

When Mai Chen was six, her family moved from Taiwan to Christchurch. This new place was strange. She knew only two words of English — watermelon and elephant. The food here was different, and any little child has trouble with that. (Remember what you were like when you were small?)

Some children made up bullying songs about the four little foreign girls. One man was so astonished to see four Chinese girls walking to the park that he drove into a car stopped at the traffic lights. (This would not have been his brightest moment.)

Mai already knew it was tough being a girl. Now it was tough being Chinese. But Mai made a decision. She would make her mark on New Zealand.

She studied hard at primary and secondary school. She did so well that she was made head girl and became Dux.

Mai studied to become a lawyer. She won scholarships and fellowships. She wrote about the Treaty of Waitangi. She worked at the United Nations in Switzerland. She came back to New Zealand to be a senior lecturer in law at Victoria University.

An ex-prime minister asked if she'd set up a law firm. It would be the first in Australasia to specialise in public law, which is about how government regulations affect people.

'Why me?' asked Mai.

'No one else would be mad enough and determined enough,' he said.

'You're on,' said Mai.

So that little girl became one of the country's top lawyers. She wrote books to help newcomers to the country understand their rights. She set up the Superdiversity Centre to help business and government with legal and business matters to do with immigrants. Mai knows the world is full of twists and turns, and encourages people to find their own opportunities.

After all, she did. And now she is celebrated for being a woman leader.

ILLUSTRATED BY Fifi Colston

Margaret Cruickshank

Doctor

1873–1918 | Born in Palmerston, New Zealand

WHEN MARGARET WAS 18, SHE DECIDED TO BECOME A DOCTOR. IN THOSE TIMES THAT WAS BRAVE OF HER.

Once, twin girls lived in the small town of Palmerston. Their mother died, and there were five younger children to be looked after.

The twins, Margaret and Christine, worked out how to manage. Margaret would go to school one day, while Christine took care of the little ones. When Margaret came home, she would teach her twin all she had learned. The next day it would be Christine's turn to run to school, and in the evening she'd teach Margaret.

When Margaret was 18, she decided to become a doctor. In those times that was brave of her — only one other woman in New Zealand was doing the same. Margaret said they never had any trouble from the male medical students, although perhaps she was being polite.

At any rate, she became the first woman in New Zealand to register as a general practitioner. She went to Waimate, where she worked as assistant to a Dr Barclay.

One year she went to Britain for more medical study. When she returned, the people of Waimate were so happy that they made her Queen of the Carnival. She wore a dress of satin, with her hair arranged like a crown.

Then World War One broke out, and Dr Barclay left to join the fighting.

Margaret was on her own. She had to rush around doing his work as well as her own, and also help run the local hospital.

The war ended, but brought no rest. In the terrible epidemic of Spanish 'flu, Margaret's driver fell ill. Between seeing patients, she had no time to sit and gather some energy. She had to cycle to visit the next patient or hurry around the district using a horse and gig.

Sometimes she found a mother too ill to feed her baby. 'I'll warm up a bottle and feed it myself,' Margaret said. She'd prepare a meal for the whole family, too.

Other times she arrived to find everyone sick. She'd simply hurry to milk the family cow so the family could have some nourishment.

So it was no surprise that Margaret caught the 'flu herself. She died of pneumonia.

In Waimate, a statue to Margaret stands like a queen. Below her is written: *Beloved Physician/Faithful unto Death*.

ILLUSTRATED BY Ali Teo

Margaret Mahy

Writer

1936–2012 | Born in Whakatāne, New Zealand

HER POWERS WERE REVEALED – SHE COULD WRITE STORIES THAT CARRIED READERS TO FANTASTICAL WORLDS.

Once upon a time a baby with mysterious powers was born in Whakatāne. Her name was Margaret. It was some years before her powers were revealed — she could write stories that carried readers to fantastical worlds.

When she was little, Margaret wanted stories to be true so badly that she tried to convince other children that she spoke the languages of animals.

Although she wanted to be a writer, she thought it would never earn much money. She had better make a living at something else. First, she tried nursing. She tried hard. But it didn't suit.

So she went to university while she thought about what to do next, and loved learning about philosophy and folk tales.

At last Margaret decided the best thing would be to get a job with books. She became a librarian.

Margaret saw everything as an adventure. For example, she said that librarians dance on a ridge — on one side there is order, on the other lies chaos.

She never married, but had two little girls. After a busy day at the library, she'd race home to cook for her daughters. She fed the dogs, cats, guinea pigs, rabbits, birds and whatever else was around at the time. Then she tucked her girls into bed.

Finally, she could rush to her desk. There, until late at night, Margaret wove her word-enchantments.

An American publisher saw some of Margaret's stories from the *School Journal*. Like a fairy godmother with money rather than magic, the publisher flew to New Zealand to examine everything Margaret had written. '*The Lion in the Meadow*! And this one, and these, must be published as books,' she declared.

Margaret's first picture books made her famous almost at once. Her first two novels each won the Carnegie Medal. But it was still a while before Margaret could afford to spend all her time writing tales of adventure and fun for children from toddlers to teenagers.

Still, she won prize after prize all over the world. The list is so long it would never fit on a page, unless the print was so small that even a mouse would have to squint.

ILLUSTRATED BY Sarah Laing

Mavis Rivers

Singer

1929–1992 | Born in Samoa;
immigrated to New Zealand in 1947

HER VOICE WAS FLOWING HONEY, LIGHT AND FULL OF MISCHIEF AND JOY.

Mavis was born in the beautiful town of Apia in beautiful Western Samoa.

Her family were all wonderful singers. At first Mavis cried as any baby does, and it cannot always have been beautiful listening. But soon, among all her 12 brothers and sisters, her voice became the most lovely of all.

Their father had the Moody Rivers Dance Band. On Fridays he organised Family Night, where each of his children had to perform. ‘Sing, Mavis — oh, she’s singing already!’

During World War Two, the family sang on Samoan radio. It was broadcast on shortwave to the American troops. ‘Guys, you gotta listen. It’s our singing mascot. It’s Mavis.’

The family moved to Auckland after the war. Mavis had a typing job during the day, but at night she sang in cabarets and on radio — Polynesian songs, love songs, pop songs, slow and fast. Her voice was flowing honey, light and full of mischief and joy. In no time at all, she was the country's favourite female singer.

Then Mavis started to listen to jazz. 'Not that rubbish,' her father said.

'But listen how the musicians improvise,' said Mavis. 'I want to do that with my voice.'

So she tried it.

'Wonderful, come and hear this!' cried more and more fans.

Even though she was told how good a singer she was already, Mavis went to study singing in the USA. Slowly, she built a career in America.

But she struck a problem. While she'd be singing, often new people would come in chattering and shouting. She might as well not be singing a note. What could she do?

A wise musician gave a tip: 'Then stop singing, Mavis.'

What?

'Sure. When the crowd's rowdy, just mouth the words. They'll think, *Huh? What's goin' on*? And it'll fall quiet. Then belt it out, Mavis. They'll listen then.'

The beautiful voice of Mavis — sad songs, funny songs, songs full of joy. She sang with great conductors and with the great Frank Sinatra. He said her voice was the purest in jazz.

You gotta listen! A little singer from Samoa is among the greatest jazz artists of all time.

ILLUSTRATED BY Vasanti Unka

Merata Mita

Film-maker

1942–2010 | Born in Maketu;
Ngāti Pikiao and Ngāi Te Rangi

IT WON'T WORK UNLESS THE STORY HAS HEART. SOUL AND HEART MUST COME FROM THE PEOPLE WHO WORK ON IT.

In Maketu in the Bay of Plenty, baby Merata was born. In the distance was the sound of waves, and birds called over the estuary. While she was growing up, Merata and her eight brothers and sisters often watched newsreels and movies projected on the walls of the wharenui.

She became a high-school teacher. Some of her students, many of them Māori, had been labelled 'unteachable'. But, as good teachers do, Merata learned, too. She found if she used film and video, it encouraged these students to say what they knew and felt by using art and drawing. Every one of them was very able.

Merata felt pulled towards using images herself. She helped a Pākehā film-maker on a documentary where Māori were interviewed. But she grew worried. Were these people being shown on film in the right way? Were they being allowed to be themselves? Did the film show the truth?

Then there were troubles at Bastion Point in Auckland.

Many years ago, Ngāti Whātua had given the waterfront land to the Crown to be used as a defence site. Now the government wanted to sell it so luxury housing could be built there. Many protestors camped on the land to stop the sale.

After 506 days of protest, the government sent in police and army trucks to end it.

Merata rushed there with a crew and filmed what happened. From this, she made a documentary, *Bastion Point: Day 507*.

During the 1981 Springbok Rugby Tour, she made *Patu!*, a documentary showing the struggles between police and protestors.

Merata went on to become the first woman in New Zealand to write and direct, on her own, a feature film, *Mauri*.

She guided young film-makers.

At last Merata became so important a film-maker that a documentary was made about her: *Rangitira: Merata Mita — Making Waves*.

Merata, great artist of film, shared her secrets. 'It doesn't matter how much money you put into a film,' she said. 'It won't work unless the story has heart. Soul and heart must come from the people who work on it.'

'Show the kids pictures of what has happened in this country,' she said. 'That's how they learn. Then they can start to talk about it.'

ILLUSTRATED BY Rebecca ter Borg

BASTIO
MAOR
STOP
MAOR
LAND.
RAB

Michelle Dickinson

Scientist

Born 1978 in the UK;
immigrated to New Zealand in 2009

NEVER EVER STOP BEING CURIOUS.

There was a girl called Michelle whose curiosity could not be quenched.

When she was still very young, her parents bought a computer.

How did it work? First, Michelle took the computer to bits. Then she taught herself to write code.

Her father was learning to be an electrical engineer. Michelle was so curious that he bought her a soldering iron so she could learn along with him.

She wanted to be a superhero when she grew up. It was dreadful to be told that this wasn't possible. But Michelle guessed she just had to accept it.

Then she discovered there was a form of engineering that was breaking things with giant hammers to figure out exactly why they broke the way they did. Find out why things break, and you discover how to make them stronger. It was like huge jigsaw puzzles on all sorts of levels.

And then she discovered the science of breaking things with diamond-tipped probes called nano-indentors. They're so small the human eye can't even see them. Yes! That job would give Michelle a million jigsaws to solve and questions to answer.

She got a job at Auckland University to start a laboratory in nano-mechanics. She made her work sound such fun that her students and other staff said she should talk in public.

Talk in public? For all Michelle's curiosity and clever mind, she had terrible stage fright. She couldn't do it.

But how great it would be to explain science to people, especially to children. Kids need to realise what fun there is in science. How she'd love to encourage them — especially girls — to become scientists, too.

Michelle had always been good at asking questions, and so she asked for advice. A public-speaking expert gave her the answer.

'Be like a superhero,' he said. 'They wear disguises. Find your own disguise when you go on stage. Then it won't be you talking, it will be — who will you be?'

'I'll be Nanogirl,' Michelle said.

Michelle runs a laboratory and teaches science at university. 'Never ever stop being curious,' she says.

Nanogirl talks on stage and TV, and makes people laugh and exclaim with delight at what she shows them about science.

'Ask questions all the time,' declares Nanogirl.

ILLUSTRATED BY Helen Taylor

nano girl

Dame Mira Szászy

Māori leader and activist

1921–2001 | Born in Waihopo, Northland; Te Aupōuri and Te Rārawa

IF OTHERS CAN DO IT, SO CAN I.

In the years between the World Wars of the first half of the twentieth century, hardship fell on the country. It was the Great Depression. In the sunny north, little Mira had only one tattered dress. The family had to scratch in the garden to find a bite to eat. But Mira was happy. Her family was Māori, English and Dalmatian, and worked in harmony. 'We were all Māori,' Mira said, 'no matter what our origins.' Parengarenga Te Hāpua, the little community, was the same — poor, happy and strong.

To give herself the courage to move to the city for her education, Mira told herself, *If others can do it, so can I.*

It can't have been easy. But she'd made up her mind.

Mira became the first Māori woman to graduate from university.

At first, she was a teacher. Mira was inspired by the Universal Declaration of Human Rights, and intended to go and work with the United Nations. But she was asked to apply for a job as a welfare officer. Now she saw that her future was to fight for human rights in her own country.

Mira turned into a whirlwind, helping set up tribal welfare committees from Wellsford to Meremere.

Soon she was working for the Māori Women's Welfare League.

The League was still fairly new, but already it was clear how much it was needed. Mira, with her own knowledge of the law and encouraged by wise kuia, worked harder than ever. The League helped give Māori women a sense of community and strength. It helped with housing, health and education. It spread a network through the country, helping women in cities, small towns and villages.

Mira spoke up for her people. Over the years she said many things, but two stand out.

First, she said loudly that women should have speaking rights on the marae. Those rights should not have been lost. Women had wisdom to share, and it was an insult to both women and men to deny this.

Second was that she loved her family, her tribe, her race, her nation and all humanity. Mira prayed that her extended family would be a new world of all creeds, all races and all nations.

ILLUSTRATED BY Sarah Wilkins

Mojo Mathers

Politician and activist

Born 1966 in England;
immigrated to New Zealand in 1981

SHE WANTED TO KEEP ARGUING FOR THE ENVIRONMENT.

Once a baby was born in London. Her parents adored her and called her Mojo. She was an active little thing. But she didn't talk.

Finally, her kindergarten teachers figured out why. Mojo was deaf. She could hear some deep sounds, but that was all.

Doctors realised that during birth her oxygen had been cut off for a while. That had damaged her hearing. They made big hearing aids for her, attached to a harness strapped around her tiny body.

As Mojo grew, she learned to lip-read — it meant she always had to see people face-on to understand them. She also learned to talk. Later on, she learned sign language.

She managed well at school, and studied mathematics at university. She grew interested in the natural world and studied conservation forestry.

When Mojo had babies of her own, she couldn't hear them if they cried. She had to check on them, again and again.

She and her family moved to Coalgate, a village near the Malvern Hills, where the lovely Waikirikiri River flowed by her home. Her children swam there and picnicked and played along its banks.

But a group of dairy farmers wanted to dam near her village, and put the river into a concrete canal.

Our beautiful river? No, thought Mojo. *It would make the river too fast and dangerous. And intensive dairy farming isn't good for the environment. Chemicals from cow pee and worse dribble through the ground and poison the river.*

With the Coalgate community, she fought the proposal. They won.

The Green Party was so impressed with Mojo that they asked her to work for them. Of course she would. She wanted to keep arguing for the environment. She wanted to argue for other issues like women's rights, and get more support for anyone with disabilities.

Mojo became the first deaf Member of Parliament in New Zealand.

'But I have to know what the other politicians are talking about in the Debating Chamber,' she said. 'So I need a sign-language interpreter, or electronic note-takers.'

There was a fuss from the Speaker of the House (who is meant to keep order) about her requests. Even though sign language was already an official language in New Zealand, along with Māori and English, it was a great fuss.

But Mojo kept arguing — and won again.

ILLUSTRATED BY Phoebe Morris

Green

Nancy Wake

Spy

1912–2011 | Born in Wellington, New Zealand

'HAH! I'VE NEVER BEEN AFRAID IN MY LIFE.'

Once upon a time a little girl was born in Wellington, youngest of six in her family. 'She has a kahu, a caul,' said the Māori midwife. 'That means she'll always be lucky.'

When Nancy was nearly two, the family moved to Australia. At 16, she ran away. First she worked as a nurse. Soon she travelled to London. She became a journalist in Europe, enjoying plenty of parties and laughter.

But she also saw the rise of Hitler in Germany, and witnessed the awful cruelties performed by his Nazi followers.

When World War Two broke out, Nancy stopped being an observer. She carried messages for the French Resistance. She smuggled food. She bought an ambulance and used it to help refugees get safely away. She helped escaped prisoners of war, too, and pilots who'd been shot down.

Nancy's life was always in danger. The Nazis hunted for her, but she kept ahead of them. 'The White Mouse has escaped us yet again!' they cried.

At last they grabbed Nancy and questioned her. For four days Nancy said nothing.

Then one of her friends tricked the Germans. 'Nancy?' he said to them. 'Heavens, she's harmless.' They let her go.

Nancy managed to get back to England, but insisted she would fight on.

The British Army trained her to be a spy. She learned survival skills, codes and radio operation, night parachuting, and how to use explosives, rifles, pistols and grenades.

Then she parachuted back into central France, with orders to organise the Maquis, the French Resistance. They thought her as fierce as five men. She led more than 7500 men in many attacks.

In a German raid, the wireless codes Nancy used had to be destroyed before the Nazis found them. It was crucial that the scattered groups of Resistance fighters had new codes, but they could only be replaced by hand delivery. Nancy said a woman would have more chance of getting through German checkpoints. She did it herself. For three days, hardly stopping, she had to cycle through rough country and over mountains.

Nancy kept fighting until France was free.

When she was 89, she was asked if she had ever been scared.

'Hah!' Nancy replied. 'I've never been afraid in my life.'

ILLUSTRATED BY Fifi Colston

Neroli Fairhall

Archer

1944–2006 | Born in Christchurch, New Zealand

NEROLI HAD GRIT AND STAMINA. SHE SMILED HER BEAUTIFUL SMILE AND DECIDED TO TRY.

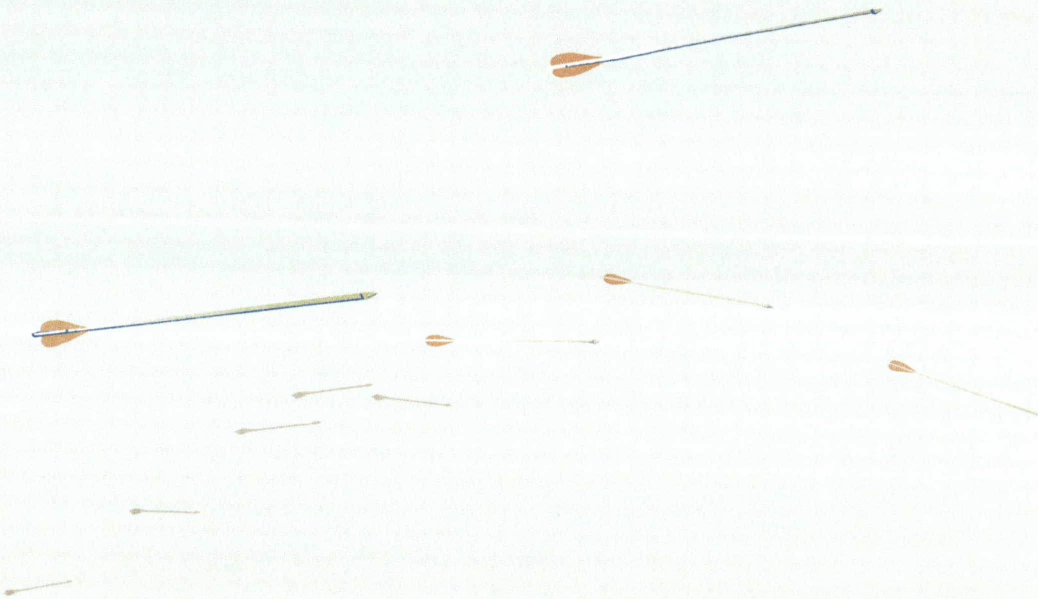

There was a young woman with a beautiful smile whose name was Neroli. She loved riding horses and motorbikes.

One day, as Neroli's bike roared over the Port Hills of Christchurch, she misjudged a turn and plunged off the road. When she was found at last, she was paralysed from the waist down. She would never walk again.

As Neroli began to recover, she made a friend, Eve. Eve had been badly hurt in an accident, too, but she'd still become a top-class athlete. 'If I can do it in a wheelchair, so can you,' she told Neroli.

Neroli had grit and stamina. She smiled her beautiful smile and decided to try.

In her wheelchair, she tried shot put, discus and wheel dashes. But they didn't suit her build.

Then Neroli tried archery. *Stance* — for her, that meant adjusting how she angled her body — *nock the arrow on the bowstring . . .*

Almost at once, this felt right for her. She had a good, straight eye. She could concentrate and stay calm. She'd have to build up strength in her arms and shoulders, but swimming would do that.

In the first national archery competition she entered, Neroli came third. She loved competing, and kept at it. *Draw and load . . .*

She won awards at Paralympic Games and international archery tournaments.

Even though she was in a wheelchair, she competed in the Commonwealth Games. The archery event was to take four days. The wind was terribly strong, but Neroli stayed calm. *Aim . . .*

And at last Neroli took the gold medal. The spectators went crazy.

Then a journalist asked, 'In the wind, is it a help or a hindrance to shoot from a wheelchair?'

'I don't know,' Neroli said. 'I've never shot standing up.'

That answer went down in sports history. And nobody thought much of the journalist.

Neroli went on to take archery titles all over the world. She was also the first paraplegic ever to compete in an Olympic Games.

At last Neroli stopped competing and took up coaching. *Release — follow through.*

ILLUSTRATED BY Rebecca ter Borg

Parris Goebel

Choreographer

Born 1991 in Manurewa, New Zealand;
Kiwi Samoan

SHE THREW HERSELF INTO HIP-HOP AS IF IT WAS FOOD FOR THE SOUL AND SHE'D BEEN STARVING.

Not long ago, baby Parris was born in Manurewa.

How that baby moved. As soon as Parris could walk, she started to dance. Her parents sent her to ballet lessons, tap-dancing and jazz ballet.

But none of those suited Parris. They were too much like following rules.

Then one day little Parris saw some hip-hop. That was it! She threw herself into hip-hop as if it was food for the soul and she'd been starving.

Five years on Parris started her own dance crew — ReQuest — with four of her friends. Her parents encouraged their dancing daughter, daughter of dance.

She choreographed the moves and trained her friends hard in her own special style: fluid, strong movements, sharp angles of the elbows and knees. Dynamic patterns full of confidence. Dancers working together like a team of warriors in glorious, urban, outrageous costumes.

Inside a year, ReQuest went to the Monsters of Hip-Hop Dance Convention in the USA. Out of thousands of dancers, Parris was chosen to perform in the finale.

She came back to school in Auckland.

Soon after, her father went to a parent-teacher interview.

'Parris needs to work harder,' the teacher said. 'She needs to show more energy.'

His daughter Parris? Who'd just proved how hard she worked at dance?

Fathers in fairy tales are sometimes harsh, or maybe they're foolish. They don't often behave like Parris's father. Nor do a lot of fathers in real life.

'Thanks, goodbye,' he said to the teacher.

Then he told Parris: 'You're leaving school. Dance is your career.'

Two years later, Parris won the Street Dance New Zealand Choreographer of the Year and the Dancer of the Year awards. She won gold in a world competition.

'What do you call your style?' a journalist asked.

Parris made a name up on the spot: 'Polyswagg.' Good one.

Now Parris directs and choreographs for stars all over the world. She's a star herself, and not just as a dancer. She's a star because she helps other young dancers find their fairy tale and — maybe — make it come true.

ILLUSTRATED BY Phoebe Morris

Patricia Grace

Writer

Born 1937 in Wellington | Ngāti Toa, Ngāti Raukawa, Te Āti Awa

PATRICIA WRITES ABOUT THE MĀORI WAY OF LIFE, ABOUT WHĀNAU AND THE POWER OF THE COMMUNITY, ABOUT LOVE.

There was once a girl called Patricia. She loved to swim and play and catch fish. On quiet days, she liked to read books. She read many books while she was growing up.

Patricia trained as a primary-school teacher, and enjoyed teaching children to read and write. Although she had seven children to take care of as well, Patricia always found time to do her own writing.

Her very first book caused a great stir. It was the first collection of short stories ever published by a Māori woman. She went on to write more short stories, and novels, as well as books for children.

The children's books have been published in Māori as well as English. With seven children, Patricia knew how to create tales for lively young minds. *The Kuia and the Spider* — an old woman and a spider have a weaving battle. *Watercress Tuna and the Children of Champion Street* — an eel with a magical throat gives children gifts that help them dance and make music. *The Trolley* — in secret, a mother makes a trolley to give to her children.

It was hard work being a teacher, a mother and finding time to write, too. Finally, Patricia decided to stop the teaching to become a full-time writer. Mother and writer? That was more than enough.

Her books for grown-ups have made her a powerful force in New Zealand writing. They're about Māori and Pākehā people coming together. They're about past injustices done to Māori by Pākehā. They are about injustices still being done to Māori. Patricia writes about the Māori way of life, about whānau and the power of the community, about love.

Patricia's writing is skilful and versatile. People find it both simple and deep, like a clear pool. She's won prizes here in New Zealand and abroad. Each book and story speaks out with a confident voice.

By the way, Patricia once said that if she weren't a writer she'd like to be a saxophone player. It's likely she'd be good at that, too.

ILLUSTRATED BY Helen Taylor

WAHINE TOA
Kuia and the

Rita Angus

Painter

1908–1970 | Born in Hastings, New Zealand

'I AM GOING TO BE FAMOUS AFTER I'VE DIED,' SHE SAID.

On a hillside in the middle of Wellington, through a small gate, lay an old cottage. The path to the door led past ferns and a hydrangea, under the cradling arms of a magnolia. Inside lived a woman with her lifetime of treasure.

Her name was Rita. People could find her difficult and cranky. She liked to be alone to keep creating more of her treasures.

But she wasn't wealthy as far as money went. The riches she made were paintings; landscapes, still lifes, portraits and self-portraits.

Corners of the tiny cottage filled up with more and more treasure.

Friends — because Rita had many friends — often asked to buy one of her pictures. 'You need the money,' they argued.

She might let them borrow a painting for a few months or even years. But she hardly ever sold one. To Rita, each artwork was a part of herself. All she cared about was sketching and painting, working on some of her canvases over and over until she was satisfied. 'I am going to be famous after I've died,' she said.

'Why don't you go overseas to get ideas?' friends sometimes asked.

'There's more than enough for me in New Zealand,' Rita said. 'It's important for me to be a woman artist in this country.'

She painted self-portraits that hold a sense of the power to be found in a woman. Three goddess pictures are symbols of peace and female strength.

When she was still young, she painted a scene that from a distance could be an angular red jewel nestling in hills. Step closer. It's the tiny railway station at Cass. The Canterbury hills reach up to hold the sky. On the edge of the platform waits a tiny figure, content with his own thoughts in the high-country air. For Rita, this painting expressed her joy in living here.

Rita thought she was born an artist. As soon as her baby fingers could hold a pencil, she'd started to draw.

She never stopped until the end of her days. Outside the cottage flowered the magnolia. Inside, bloomed Rita's treasures.

ILLUSTRATED BY Sarah Wilkins

Ruia Morrison

Tennis player

Born 1936 in Tikitere | Te Arawa,
Ngāti Tūwharetoa

'I NEVER MINDED LOSING. IF YOU LOSE IT DOESN'T MEAN THE OTHER PERSON'S BETTER. IT JUST MEANS YOU DIDN'T DO IT RIGHT.'

There was a little girl in Rotorua who forever ran about with a stick in her hand. Her name was Ruia. She swished at anything — a stone, a weed, a gatepost. If she missed, she'd double back and swish again.

When she was eight, new tennis courts opened near her home. The racquets made a wonderful sound — oh, such music — when they hit the balls. *Thwack! Pop — thwock*.

What a pest Ruia became. She was too young to play herself, but she would run behind the players. Any balls they missed, she'd belt them hard. 'Clear off,' they used to yell. 'You're in our way!'

With a cheeky smile, Ruia simply ran to the next court and did the same.

At last her dad built Ruia her own volley board at home. He painted it green with a white line to show how high the tennis net came.

'Practise on this,' he said. 'Show me you're good enough. Then you can play on the courts.'

Thwack. Thwock. By the time Ruia was 10, her father said, 'Okay, you're good enough now.'

As soon as she was on the courts, Ruia showed she was far better than simply good enough.

Very soon she was playing in championships. Her smile and personality made people notice her. It meant women's tennis began to be noticed as well.

Ruia went to train as a teacher, but she kept playing tennis. She won her first national title and people raised money to send her overseas for more experience.

Ruia was the first Māori and the first New Zealand woman to play at Wimbledon, the great tennis tournament where the fans eat strawberries and — *thwock*! — royalty comes to watch and cheer. *Thwack-pop-thwack*.

The cheeky girl forever swishing a stick is one of the greatest players in the history of New Zealand tennis.

'But I wasn't special,' Ruia says. 'Other people helped my gift to blossom. And I never minded losing. If you lose it doesn't mean the other person's better. It just means you didn't do it right.'

So — *thwock!* — you try again.

ILLUSTRATED BY Sarah Laing

Selina Tusitala Marsh

Poet

Born 1971 in Auckland, New Zealand;
Kiwi Samoan

HER OLDER BROTHER TOLD HER, 'OPEN EVERY DOOR THAT YOU FIND AJAR.'

When Selina was little, her mother would give her 50 cents. Selina would dash to an op shop. There she'd cram a cardboard box with books. Cookery books. Stories. Children's annuals. No matter what it was, Selina loved to read.

Her mother had to teach herself English when she moved from Samoa to New Zealand, but Selina soon grew clever with words. She began writing poems.

She went on with her studies. Sometimes she doubted herself. But Luka, her older brother, told her, 'Open every door that you find ajar.'

Her love of poetry grew stronger. She studied the first five Pasifika women poets to publish in English. Selina realised that writing down what you saw, thought and felt was an act of strength. She kept working on her own poems.

Selina's first book of poetry was *Fast Talking PI*. It won two awards. The poem 'Fast Talking PI' is a chant that celebrates how varied and full of energy — or sometimes quietness — Pasifika people are. When Selina reads it to school children, they chant lines they make up themselves.

When Selina was made Commonwealth Poet it was a great honour. But now she had to write a poem about unity and perform it in front of Queen Elizabeth.

Uh-oh.

But this was a big door ajar. She had better open it.

Selina wrote about the environment and bees and currents of humanity, she wrote about you and me, unity.

She packed a dress as blue as the Pacific Ocean to wear on the day. Then she travelled to London.

In empty Westminster Abbey, where she would perform, she rehearsed 'Unity'. She read it to the statues, the tombs of queens and kings, even the trees outside. But she still needed to rehearse in front of a person. And it would be best if the person wouldn't be critical.

The guardsmen outside Buckingham Palace aren't allowed to react at all when anyone talks to them. Selina walked up to one. She explained who she was, then recited 'Unity.'

'Thank you,' she said when she'd finished.

The guardsman gave the merest twitch of his eye, and she knew he'd loved it.

ILLUSTRATED BY Ali Teo

Sophie Pascoe

Swimmer

Born 1993 in Christchurch, New Zealand

If Sophie said, 'I can't do that,' they'd say, 'Why not try it and see?'

Once there was a two-year-old called Sophie, who was as lively and full of beans as two-year-olds are meant to be. She lived near Christchurch city. One day, when her dad was using the ride-on lawn mower, Sophie ran after it and he didn't see her. There was a terrible accident to the little girl's legs.

Her dad rushed Sophie to hospital. The surgeons saved her right leg though it had bad scars. Her left leg had to be amputated below the knee.

The family was devastated.

But when Sophie began to recover, her mum and dad and her loving big sister decided it would be wrong to let her doubt herself. They'd treat her just like they had before.

If Sophie said, 'I can't do that,' they'd say, 'Why not try it and see?'

Nine times out of ten, Sophie could do whatever it was.

Even before she had an artificial leg fitted, Sophie brimmed over with beans again — scrambling around, climbing jungle gyms, getting into mischief, powering on.

She started school. With her artificial leg, she ran in a five-year-old's race — and came first against all the kids who had two whole legs.

Then Sophie wanted to try swimming. At first all the other kids were better than her. Her mum hunted out a good coach to help.

The very first race Sophie entered after that, she won.

Her swimming career started powering on.

By the time Sophie was nine, her grandad asked her to make him a promise: *When you're older, compete in the Paralympics and win a gold medal*.

For six more years, Sophie trained. Often she was exhausted. Sometimes her injuries still hurt. She kept powering on.

At last she was selected to swim for New Zealand at the Paralympic Games. She won a gold medal. Oh, wait — make that three gold medals and a silver.

She won more medals in later Paralympics. She's also won gold and silver medals in World Championships and the Commonwealth Games.

Sophie has changed the way people think about para sport. And so far she has won nine gold medals for her grandad, and that's only counting from the Paralympics.

ILLUSTRATED BY Phoebe Morris

Suzanne Aubert

Missionary

1835–1926 | Born in Loire, France; immigrated to New Zealand in 1860

'NO, THANK YOU,' SHE SAID. 'I'M SERVING GOD HERE.'

One day in France, little Suzanne fell through the ice onto some rocks. She was rescued, but she was lame and blind.

Slowly, Suzanne recovered. And she decided: *All my life, I'll serve the sick and disabled.*

Finally, her parents said Suzanne was to be married.

'No, thank you,' she replied. 'I will serve God.'

So she trained as a nurse, became a Catholic missionary and sailed to New Zealand. But she discovered she was expected to teach singing and needlework to well-off city girls. Was that the best way to serve God?

Certainly not, thought Suzanne.

Instead, she worked with Māori girls. In almost no time, she spoke Māori well.

After a while a new bishop told Suzanne to return to France.

'No, thank you,' she said. 'I'm serving God here.'

She travelled to the Hawke's Bay and worked there with the Catholic Māori mission. She learned from Māori women about local plants and herbs, and began making her own medicines.

Next Suzanne travelled up the Whanganui River to Jerusalem. This mission was far from anywhere, and hard to manage. It led to arguments with Church leaders.

To get around some of the rules, Suzanne became a Religious Sister and set up a new religious Order, the Daughters of Our Lady of Compassion. It helped ailing old folk, homeless Pākehā children and anyone in need.

At last Suzanne decided the Daughters of Our Lady of Compassion should work in Wellington with disabled people, working mothers and orphans.

'You can't do this and that, nor that and this,' the Government said. 'What's more, there's a new law about medicines. Nobody can use potions they've made themselves.'

Very well, Suzanne decided, she'd stop making hers.

But the Government kept complaining about that and this.

Church leaders chimed in as well. 'Don't do this other thing. Nor that one. As for those things, certainly not.'

Suzanne decided this time she'd ask for help so she could keep serving God. So she travelled to Rome and asked the Pope to recognise her Order. And he did. Then the Church in New Zealand could no longer try to boss her about.

Dame Suzie Moncrieff

Sculptor and arts entrepreneur

Born 1949 in Hope, New Zealand

**SHE KEPT THINKING,
IF I JUST STICK AT IT A BIT LONGER,
WILL IT BE MORE SUCCESSFUL?**

Suzie's mother painted, acted and sang. Suzie's father had a dance band. Little Suzie wrote her own plays and painted the sets. When she grew up she wanted to be an artist and sculptor. So she applied to art school. But the art school said *no*.

Suzie thought she'd be a teacher instead. When she tried that, it didn't feel right. So she said *no*.

Finally she thought, *But what if I try sculpting anyway?*

With six other artists, she opened a gallery near Nelson. She ran a sculpture competition so people would hear where the gallery was. That worked, for a short while.

What if there was something totally new? Suzie thought. *What if art could move? What if people could wear it? What if they could even dance in it, with great music and beautiful lights?*

It was a risk. But she organised a wearable art show in the gallery. The audience was 200 people. Not bad for a first time.

Next year the audience was bigger. The next year — bigger again. But it was still a risk and cost Suzie heaps of money. She kept thinking, *If I just stick at it a bit longer, will it be more successful?*

She stuck at it. And from all over New Zealand artists and designers began to create entries for Suzie's World of WearableArt Show.

The show grew so popular and so big that it had to move from Nelson to Wellington.

Now, entries come to the World of WearableArt from all over the world. Artists work for months or even years hoping win a place in the show. Suzie has to hire hundreds of fabulous musicians, lighting and sound technicians, models and dancers. The show lasts for nearly three weeks with several categories. The audience is tens of thousands of people, clapping and cheering at the parade of imagination, colour and movement.

Suzie's won many awards for her brilliant idea. But the best one has to be when Massey University made her an honorary Doctor in Fine Arts.

Remember the art school that said *no*?

Suzie gave the best answer to that when she thought, *But — what if . . .* ?

ILLUSTRATED BY Fifi Colston

Te Puea Herangi

Māori leader

1883–1952 | Born in Whatiwhatihoe;
Ngāti Mahuta, Pākehā,
Ngāti Ngāwaero, Ngāti Maniopoto

SHE MAY NOT HAVE WANTED TO BE CALLED A PRINCESS, BUT SHE BEHAVED AS A STRONG PRINCESS SHOULD.

Mount Pirongia in the Waikato is often wreathed with a coronet of mist. Near there, Te Puea was born to the daughter of the second Māori King, Tāwhiao Te Wherowhero, and his wife, Hera.

As this tiny girl grew up, she was educated in Māori ways. But when she was a teenager she was often sick. She thought her life would be short, and so decided to have a good time while she could. Te Puea ran away.

There had been difficult years after the New Zealand Wars, and the Tainui people's land had been confiscated. Te Puea's uncle believed that she had great abilities and could help with this. Finally he called her back.

'Remember your duty to your people,' he said.

Te Puea listened. At first she was reluctant, but she agreed. She would try to be a leader. She'd try to bring people together. Her love of laughter might be a help.

She had many arguments with the government of the time. But she did what she could. She composed waiata that told of injustice. She gathered up 100 orphans who needed to be cared for. She arranged for a carved meeting house to be built to help people be proud.

Gradually Te Puea became friends with the Prime Minister. A leading journalist wrote about her work helping the poor. In the articles they called her Princess.

'I am not,' Te Puea said. 'There is no princess in Māoritanga.'

She continued to have arguments with the government. But they awarded her a medal, then two years later another one. It puzzled her — but maybe it meant she was doing good work.

And she worked on using traditional ways, dance, story and song to bring people together. Finally she agreed with the government on payment for the confiscated land.

All the time Te Puea never forgot how important it was to laugh. Having fun brought people together, young or old, rich or poor, Māori or Pākehā.

She may not have wanted to be called a princess, but she behaved as a strong princess should.

ILLUSTRATED BY Sarah Wilkins

Dame Valerie Adams

Athlete

Born 1984 in Rotorua, New Zealand;
Kiwi Tongan

JUST KEEP GOING,

SHE ALWAYS TOLD HERSELF.

Valerie was a champion. For more than 11 years she'd competed at shot put, sometimes winning, other times not. By now she had 14 gold medals and many silver and bronze. She knew you could never count on success. It takes constant battle to do your best.

Shot put is hard. *Just keep going,* Valerie always told herself.

Throwing the shot was second nature by now, but she still checked her routine. Lifted the shot over her head. Brought it straight down under her jaw. Pushed it into her neck, elbow parallel to the ground . . .

One of Valerie's rivals was Nadzeya. Sometimes Valerie beat her. Other times Nadzeya won.

The Olympic Games were coming up. Valerie had just won the World Championship with a personal best throw. She was feeling strong. But in sport, you can't stop training. She worked especially hard.

In the weeks of practice leading up to the Games, Nadzeya began throwing the shot longer and longer distances. Valerie trained even harder. She did weights to make her legs and arms more powerful. She imagined her whole body as a cannon propelling the shot.

On the day of the contest, Valerie used all of her knowledge of being a champion to stay calm and drive the shot as far as she could.

Nadzeya won.

Valerie hid her disappointment. After all, she'd won the silver medal and silver is great.

But sports commentators said: *Is it time Valerie stopped competing? Is it time she retired?*

No way, Valerie thought. She'd just prove how good she was at the next Olympics. All she had to do was train harder.

'I'll retire when I'm ready,' she told her coach.

'Good on you,' he said.

Then one week after the Olympics Valerie had a phone call from a sports official.

'Nadzeya has failed a drug test,' he said. 'She has been disqualified. She loses the gold medal. The gold is yours.'

Whether someone else had slipped the drug into Nadzeya's food or she'd taken it herself — it didn't matter. She'd had artificial help to win the competition.

Valerie's disappointment turned to disbelief. Disbelief bloomed into joy.

Valerie the champion had won gold again after all.

ILLUSTRATED BY Sophie Watson

Dame Whina Cooper

Māori leader and activist

1895–1994 | Born in Te Karaka, Hokianga; Te Rārawa and Taranaki

THE ENTIRE NATION WATCHED THIS REMARKABLE WOMAN AT THE FOREFRONT OF A PROTEST.

Long ago in northern Hokianga, lively baby Whina first saw the sky. She lived in the tiny settlement of Panguru. When she was seven, she used to walk to school nearly 10 kilometres away. And back again.

Whina became interested in finding ways to help her community. She became a teacher at the Pawarenga Native School. She took part in a protest to stop farmers draining a swamp that Māori had used to gather seafood whenever it flooded. When she married, she worked even harder for her community. Her skill was getting people to work together. Very soon she was a leader in land development. She became a great speaker, encouraging others.

Her children needed secondary schooling, so Whina moved to Auckland. There, too, she worked hard for Māori people, and became the first president of the Māori

Women's Welfare League. With her great oratory she shone a light on the needs of Māori women and children in particular. She worked and worked while she grew old.

At last the Queen awarded Whina a medal for all her work. She accepted the honour humbly. 'I am the wearer to show that if some can get to these heights, we all can,' Whina said. Now she thought she could rest at last and other kuia would take over.

But a knock came on her door.

Groups of people had joined together to form Te Rōpū o te Matakite, to protest more land loss. Would Whina lead them?

She was 80 years old. But she was still bright and lively in the ways that mattered.

Whina led a land march 10,000 kilometres, from Te Hāpua in the Far North to Parliament in Wellington. The entire nation watched this remarkable woman at the forefront of a protest that made it clear how determined Māori were to keep their land and culture.

Now Whina was given more honours. She was made a Dame of the British Empire, then a Member of the Order of New Zealand.

Even in her last years, Whina's message was always that the nation should be united. She died back in her beloved Hokianga when she was 98.

More than a million Māori and Pākehā wept together.

ILLUSTRATED BY Sarah Laing

Yvette Williams

Athlete

Born 1929 in Dunedin, New Zealand

SHE WAS THE GOLDEN GIRL OF NEW ZEALAND SPORT.

There was a mother who was a champion highland dancer. The father was a champion at throwing grenades (although he never tried that at home). The brother and sister hurdled and wrestled on the front lawn. The girl, Yvette, could run from the doorway of her bedroom and leap right onto the top bunk. She learned to jump over her grandfather's flower bed (partly because she didn't dare land in the middle).

But Yvette never played actual sport until she was 18 and joined an athletics club.

Only two months later, Yvette won the shot put at the New Zealand athletics championships. She also won for tossing the javelin. And for discus and for long jump and for hurdles.

This all-round girl needed a really good coach. So her parents found one. He made Yvette jump from the top of the dunes at St Clair Beach, near Dunedin. He made her wear heavy army boots for running. Then when Yvette took them off, she felt as light as if she were flying.

Soon she was the golden girl of New Zealand sport. She won the long jump in the British Empire Games. She won again at the Olympic Games in Finland.

By the time Yvette arrived home after the Olympics, it was weeks after her win. Surely the fuss would be over by now?

Her plane landed in Auckland. Her parents were waiting to drive her all the way back home to Dunedin.

But first she was whisked away in a limousine to Western Springs where a huge crowd waited for her. There was a display of fireworks. Everyone shouted, 'Congratulations, Golden Girl!'

Her parents drove her down to Wellington. She was invited to Parliament to shake hands with the Prime Minister. Surely the fuss was over now?

They drove down the South Island. In every town, groups of children and their parents waved flags and offered Yvette bunches of flowers.

And in Dunedin Yvette had to sit in a big, open car. Down the main street it drove, under bunting and flags, while the crowds cheered.

'Our Golden Girl! Welcome home.'

ILLUSTRATED BY *Vasanti Unka*

Epic Go Girls

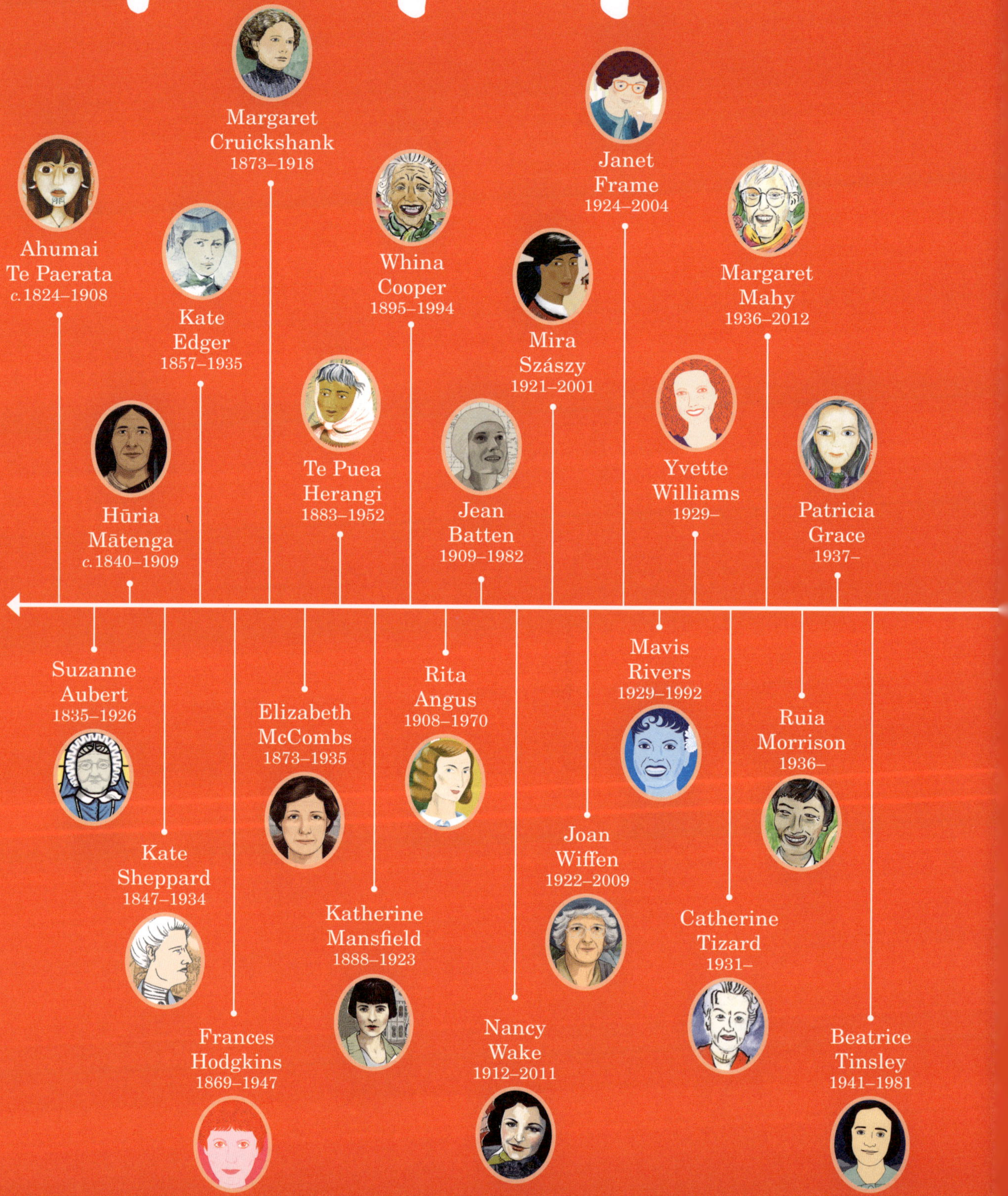

Through History

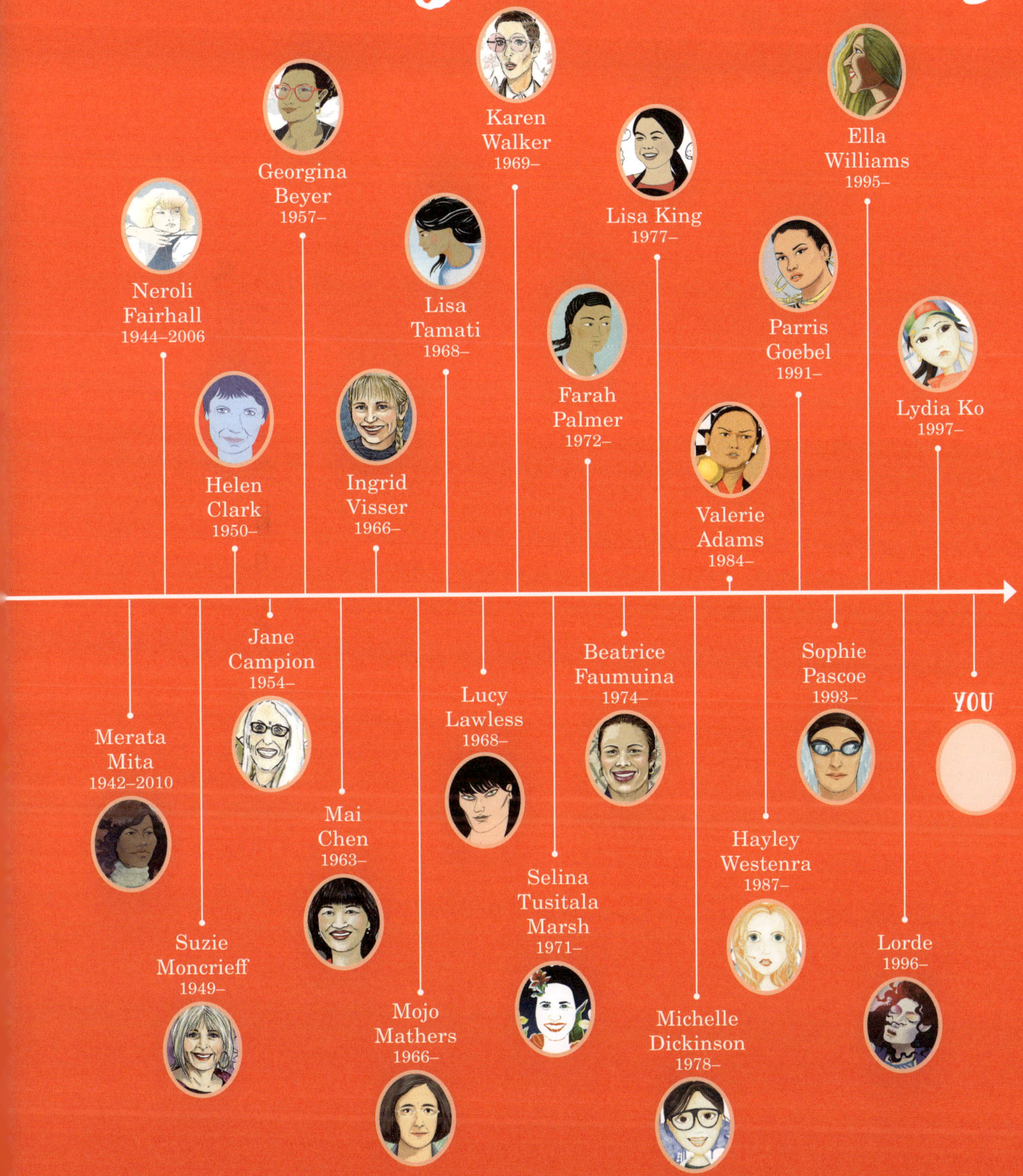

About the Author

Barbara Else
is a writer and editor, born in Invercargill. She has lived in Wellington, Auckland, Oamaru, Christchurch, Dunedin and San Diego. At school she became a bookworm; with her head always in a novel, a Superman comic or an encyclopaedia. She was very shy except for when she wrote plays for her class to perform. Barbara wanted to be an actor or perhaps a radio journalist. At university she studied English Literature and History.

She was surprised to begin writing her own stories but found it great fun. She's published many novels for adults and children, and has edited several story collections for children.

She has won fellowships and prizes and is a Member of the New Zealand Order of Merit for services to literature. She also has the Margaret Mahy Medal for children's literature.

She can still be shy but gets a kick from a bit of stage fright.

About the Illustrators

Ali Teo

When she was young, Ali loved to draw. Then she grew up and realised you could make a living from art, so she went to design school and learnt the tricks of the trade. Now she gets to work from home, draw all sorts of interesting things, and can wear her pjs all day if she wants to.

Fifi Colston

was born in Yorkshire, lived in Africa, then in New Zealand. As a little girl she drew and made things and dreamed of being a creative artist. She now lives in Wellington and is one, every single delicious day!

Helen Taylor

was born in the South Island town of Oamaru. Having a flair for drawing, she dreamt that one day she might be a book illustrator. She kept on drawing, because she realised that Kiwi girls can do anything when they grow up. She now works as an artist and writer, and lives in a bright yellow house with her two children and too many cats, in Lyttelton.

About the Illustrators

Sarah Laing
was born in Champaign-Urbana in the USA, but promptly moved to Palmerston North. She had lots of ideas as to what she was going to be when she grew up — a gypsy fortune teller, a circus performer, a vet, an international woman of mystery. She is still surprised to find herself as a writer and illustrator living in Wellington.

Phoebe Morris
was born in Wellington and grew up there in the windy weather. As a young girl, Phoebe dreamed of being a zookeeper and looking after animals. Because she was allergic to animals, she ended up drawing them instead. Now Phoebe works as an illustrator and gets to draw animals and more every day.

Sophie Watson
was born and raised in Auckland, and couldn't wait to leave. After exploring a few corners of the globe she is now happily back in her hometown, where she spends her days making art, helping others to make art and having conversations with her cats.

About the Illustrators

Sarah Wilkins
was born in Lower Hutt. The middle child of seven, she dreamt of becoming a solo explorer. Dreaming and drawing, which she loved, go together, so she became an illustrator instead. Sarah lives in Wellington, and sometimes Paris, and likes to explore everything in between.

Rebecca ter Borg
As a young girl living in Rotorua, Rebecca's ambition was to be 'a starving artist living in an attic'. Luckily she is not starving and lives on a ground-level house in Auckland with her two daughters, but she does work as an illustrator and still loves drawing as much as she did back then.

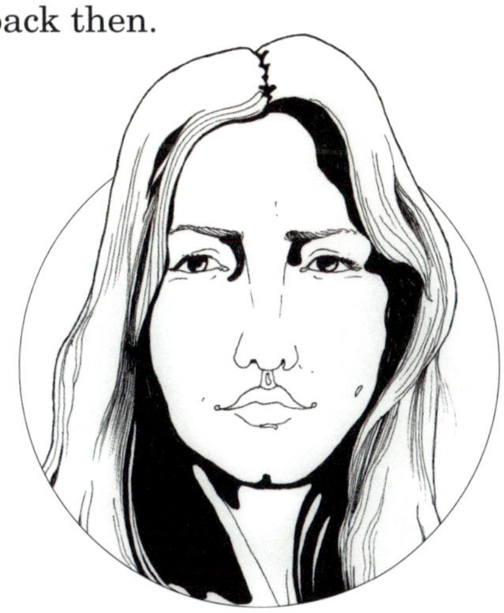

Vasanti Unka
was born in Pukekohe. She wanted to do something exciting. She imagined being a racing-car driver. She drew endless pictures of cars and glued them into tiny books she made herself. Nowadays, Vasanti drives too slowly to be a racer; she finds far more excitement in illustrating, designing and writing books.

Now you've read *Go Girl,* you might like to learn more about these heroes and their careers. Ask your local or school librarian — there are some wonderful books written about (or even by) these epic women. You can also look them up online in *Te Ara, the Encyclopedia of New Zealand*. It includes the *Dictionary of New Zealand Biography*. www.teara.govt.nz.

PUFFIN

UK | USA | Canada | Ireland | Australia
India | New Zealand | South Africa | China

Puffin is an imprint of the Penguin Random House group of companies,
whose addresses can be found at global.penguinrandomhouse.com.
First published by Penguin Random House New Zealand, 2018

Penguin Random House New Zealand

5 7 9 10 8 6 4

The stories in *Go Girl* are not comprehensive biographies; they are creative non-fiction pieces written to inspire the imagination of a young audience. The publisher and author were solely responsible for the selection of women and none of the subjects has an association, commercial or otherwise, with the book.

Cover illustration by Vasanti Unka © Penguin Random House New Zealand
Text design by Rachel Clark © Penguin Random House New Zealand
Author portrait by Vasanti Unka
Prepress by Image Centre Group
Printed and bound in China by RR Donnelley Asia Printing Solutions Ltd

A catalogue record for this book is available from the National Library of New Zealand.

ISBN 978-0-14-377160-9

creative nz
Arts Council of New Zealand Toi Aotearoa

penguin.co.nz

FSC www.fsc.org
MIX
Paper from responsible sources
FSC® C101537